Olga Khomenko

Ukrainians beyond Borders
Nine Life Journeys Through the History of Eastern Europe

With a foreword by Zbigniew Wojnowski

UKRAINIAN VOICES

Collected by Andreas Umland

77 *Viktoriia Grivina*
    Kharkiv—A War City
    A Collection of Essays from 2022–23
    ISBN 978-3-8382-1988-2

78 *Hjørdis Clemmensen, Viktoriia Grivina,*
    Vasylysa Shchogoleva
    Kharkiv Is a Dream
    Public Art and Activism 2013–2023
    With a foreword by Bohdan Volynskyi
    ISBN 978-3-8382-2005-5

79 *Olga Khomenko*
    The Faraway Sky of Kyiv
    Ukrainians in the War
    With a foreword by Hiroaki Kuromiya
    ISBN 978-3-8382-2006-2

80 *Daria Mattingly, Jonathon Vsetecka (eds.)*
    The Holodomor in Global Perspective
    How the Famine in Ukraine Shaped the World
    With a foreword by Anne Applebaum
    ISBN 978-3-8382-1953-0

The book series "Ukrainian Voices" publishes English- and German-language monographs, edited volumes, document collections, and anthologies of articles authored and composed by Ukrainian politicians, intellectuals, activists, officials, researchers, and diplomats. The series' aim is to introduce Western and other audiences to Ukrainian explorations, deliberations and interpretations of historic and current, domestic, and international affairs. The purpose of these books is to make non-Ukrainian readers familiar with how some prominent Ukrainians approach, view and assess their country's development and position in the world. The series was founded, and the volumes are collected by Andreas Umland, Dr. phil. (FU Berlin), Ph. D. (Cambridge), Associate Professor of Politics at the Kyiv-Mohyla Academy and an Analyst in the Stockholm Centre for Eastern European Studies at the Swedish Institute of International Affairs.

Olga Khomenko

UKRAINIANS BEYOND BORDERS
Nine Life Journeys Through the History of Eastern Europe

With a foreword by Zbigniew Wojnowski

Bibliografische Information der Deutschen Nationalbibliothek
Die Deutsche Nationalbibliothek verzeichnet diese Publikation in der Deutschen Nationalbibliografie; detaillierte bibliografische Daten sind im Internet über http://dnb.d-nb.de abrufbar.

Bibliographic information published by the Deutsche Nationalbibliothek
The Deutsche Nationalbibliothek lists this publication in the Deutsche Nationalbibliografie; detailed bibliographic data are available on the Internet at http://dnb.d-nb.de.

Cover picture: ID 174671995 © Hel080808 | Dreamstime.com

ISBN (Print): 978-3-8382-2007-9
ISBN (E-Book [PDF]): 978-3-8382-8007-3
© *ibidem*-Verlag, Hannover • Stuttgart 2025

Leuschnerstraße 40
30457 Hannover
Germany / Deutschland
info@ibidem.eu

Alle Rechte vorbehalten

Das Werk einschließlich aller seiner Teile ist urheberrechtlich geschützt. Jede Verwertung außerhalb der engen Grenzen des Urheberrechtsgesetzes ist ohne Zustimmung des Verlages unzulässig und strafbar. Dies gilt insbesondere für Vervielfältigungen, Übersetzungen, Mikroverfilmungen und elektronische Speicherformen sowie die Einspeicherung und Verarbeitung in elektronischen Systemen.

All rights reserved. No part of this publication may be reproduced, stored in or introduced into a retrieval system, or transmitted, in any form, or by any means (electronic, mechanical, photocopying, recording or otherwise) without the prior written permission of the publisher. Any person who commits any unauthorized act in relation to this publication may be liable to criminal prosecution and civil claims for damages.

Printed in the EU

Contents

List of Figures 7

Foreword by *Zbigniew Wojnowski* 9

Introduction 11

Acknowledgment 17

An Itinerant Freethinker: Hryhorii Skovoroda 21

Ilya Mechnikov: A Founding Figure in Immunology and Gerontology 29

The Last Romantic in Exile:
Serhii Bortkevych/Sergei Bortkiewicz 41

The Poetry of Colour: The Vibrant World of Sonia Delaunay 55

A Statesman of Conscience: Mykhailo Tereshchenko 67

From Imagination to Flight: The Life of Igor Sikorsky 87

Ukrainian Dreams on the Pacific Rim: Ivan Svit's Far Eastern Mission 97

Across Continents, Toward Japan: The Life of Stepan Levynskyi/Stefan Lewinski 113

Ukraine's Marco Polo: The Global Journey of Sofia Yablonska-Oudin 127

A Prince by Birth, a Ukrainian by Choice: Vasyl Vyshyvanyi Archduke Wilhelm Franz von Habsburg-Lothringen 139

Conclusion: Borders and Beyond: The Ukrainian Spirit 145

Historical Timeline 161

Selected Bibliography 167

List of Figures

Figure 1. Portrait of Hryhorii Skovoroda, nineteenth century, artist unknown. Source: "Hryhorii Skovoroda," Wikipedia.
https://en.wikipedia.org/wiki/Hryhorii_Skovoroda#/media/File:%D0%93%D1%80%D0%B8%D0%B3%D0%BE%D1%80%D0%B8%D0%B9_%D0%A1%D0%BA%D0%BE%D0%B2%D0%BE%D1%80%D0%BE%D0%B4%D0%B0.jpg

Figure 2. Ilya Mechnikov, ca. 1910–1915; photographer unknown. Source: "Élie Metchnikoff," Wikipedia.
https://en.wikipedia.org/wiki/%C3%89lie_Metchnikoff#/media/File:Elie_Metchnikoff_-_Between_ca._1910_and_ca._1915_-_LOC.jpg

Figure 3. Serhii Bortkevych, date unknown; photographer unknown. Source: "Sergei Bortkiewicz," Olympedia.
https://www.olympedia.org/athletes/2000528

Figure 4. Sonia Delaunay wearing Casa Sonia creations, Madrid, c.1920; photographer unknown. Source: "Sonia Delaunay," Wikipedia.
https://en.wikipedia.org/wiki/Sonia_Delaunay#/media/File:Sonia_Delaunay_wearing_Casa_Sonia_creations,_Madrid,_c.1920.jpg

Figure 5. Mykhailo Tereshchenko, c.1917; photographer unknown. Source: "Mikhail Tereshchenko," Wikipedia.
https://en.wikipedia.org/wiki/Mikhail_Tereshchenko#/media/File:Mikhail_Ivanovich_Tereshchenko.jpg

Figure 6. Igor Sikorsky, c.1914; photographer unknown. Source: "Igor Sikorsky," Igor Sikorsky Kyiv Polytechnic Institute.
https://kpi.ua/en/2021-sikorsky

Figure 7. Igor Sikorsky; photographer unknown. Source: "Igor Sikorsky," Encyclopædia Britannica.
https://www.britannica.com/biography/Igor-Sikorsky

Figure 8. Ivan Svit. Source: Olha Khomenko, The Far Eastern Odyssey of Ivan Svit (Kyiv: Laurus, 2021). Permission to me from Ukrainian Academy or Arts and Science in USA (UVAN)

Figure 9. Stepan Levynskyi, c. early 20th century; photographer unknown. Source: Sofia Yablonska Foundation — permission to me.

Figure 10. Sofia Yablonska and her husband Jean Oudind, c. early 20th century; photographer unknown. Source: Sofia Yablonka foundation — permission to me.

Figure 11. Sofia Yablonska with a camera, c. 1930s; photographer unknown. Source: Sofia Yablonska Foundation — permission to me.

Figure 12. Sofia Yablonska; photographer unknown. Source: Sofia Yablonska Foundation—permission to me

Figure 13. Archduke Wilhelm of Austria, c.1918; photographer unknown. Source: "Archduke Wilhelm of Austria," Wikipedia. https://en.wikipedia.org/wiki/Archduke_Wilhelm_of_Austria#/media/File:Vyshyvanyi_01.jpg

Figure 14. Kazimir Huzhkovsky and Archduke Wilhelm of Austria, c.1918; photographer unknown. Source: Wikimedia Commons. https://uk.m.wikipedia.org/wiki/%D0%A4%D0%B0%D0%B9%D0%BB:Guzhkovsky_and_Habsburg.jpg

Foreword

Olga Khomenko's research spans an impressive range of topics and geographical regions. She has published widely on postwar Japan, Ukrainian migration in the Far East, and Ukraine-Japan relations. Over the past decade, Khomenko has played a leading role in introducing Japanese readers to Ukrainian history and culture, helping foster dialogue between the two countries at a critical juncture.

Ukrainians beyond Borders. Nine Life Journeys Through the History of Eastern Europe is an English edition of Khomenko's book which has won widespread acclaim since its publication in Japan in February 2022. It follows the fascinating biographies of scientists, engineers, artists, social activists, and political leaders who travelled the world and put Ukraine on the map between the 18th and 20th centuries. The identities and mindsets of Khomenko's protagonists are difficult to pin down. Most were born in the multi-ethnic territories of what is today Ukraine. Others, like Vasyl Vysyvanyi, adopted Ukraine as a homeland later in life. They all came of age when state borders and ethnic identities were in flux. Their travels between Ukraine and the Tsarist and Habsburg capitals, as well as their illustrious careers across Europe, North America, and East Asia, provide rich insights into the shifting meanings of borders, changing imperial hierarchies, and ultimately the emergence of modern Ukrainian nationhood.

Khomenko's transnational approach demonstrates that the history of modern Ukraine does not have to be confined to the boundaries of Tsarist Russia, the Habsburg Empire, or the Soviet Union. Rather, Ukraine can and should be studied as part of global history. The men and women described in this book left an important imprint on the international art scene, new technologies, and fashion trends. Others—like Sofia Yablonska-Oudin—were pioneers of cultural and public diplomacy. Equally important, Khomenko's protagonists are part of the global history of imperialism, settler colonialism, and great power politics in the wake of World War I. At a time when many scholars of Eastern Europe seek to move beyond Russocentric narratives, histories of travel can highlight the key role of the so-called "peripheries" in modern global history.

The book draws on well-known studies of modern Ukrainian history in English, but also introduces us to materials which are perhaps more difficult to access, including primary sources and scholarship in Ukrainian and Japanese. Whereas the history of Ukrainian diaspora communities in the broadly conceived "West" is relatively well-known, Khomenko also devotes attention to Ukrainian connections with Asia. In this way, the book shows that there is great potential in moving beyond the narrative of Ukraine as a "borderland" between the East and West.

Nine Life Journeys Through the History of Eastern Europe is a timely publication which responds to the increased interest in Ukraine following the full-scale Russian invasion in 2022. At the same time, Khomenko shows that the history of Eastern Europe is more than just war and suffering. In highlighting Ukraine's transnational entanglements, the book raises the hope that the region will remain part of global history long after the current war is over.

Zbigniew Wojnowski
Associate Professor of Soviet History
St Antony's College
University of Oxford
United Kingdom

Introduction

This book was born amid profound global upheaval—the COVID-19 pandemic that began in 2019—and first reached Japanese readers just weeks before the full-scale Russian invasion of Ukraine in February 2022. At first, my aim was simple: to inspire and uplift readers stuck at home, unable to travel, by sharing the stories of Ukrainians who made their mark far beyond their homeland. I could never have imagined—nor wished in my darkest thoughts—that mere weeks after publication, millions of Ukrainians would be crossing borders not as travellers but as refugees, fleeing a war that has since reshaped their country and the world.

Tragically, this is not a new experience for Ukraine. Situated on open plains with few natural defenses like mountains or seas, Ukraine has long been vulnerable to invasion. From the Russian Revolution and World War I to the shifting regimes of the 20th-century, its people have endured war, displacement, and imposed borders time and again. These experiences have forged a nation deeply familiar with both loss and resilience—people who, even when forced to begin again, find the continuing strength to rebuild.

Today, as in generations past, Ukrainians—mostly women and children—are leaving behind homes and livelihoods in search of safety. They face the immense challenge of remaking their lives in unfamiliar lands, carrying the burdens of war while also seeking new purpose and strength.

This book is a testament to that enduring spirit. It explores the lives of ten individuals born in Ukraine between the 18th and 20th centuries—artists, scientists, diplomats, and thinkers—whose achievements resonated far beyond national borders. Their stories illuminate what it means to be shaped by Ukrainian lands and traditions, even while crossing into other worlds.

Many readers may already know names like Mykola Hohol/Nikolai Gogol (1809-1852), the writer from Poltava, or Serhii Korolyov/Sergei Korolyov (1907-1966), the space pioneer born in Zhytomyr, or Ilya Repin (1844-1930), famous painter of Cossack descent from Kharkiv gubernia. Others might be surprised to learn that the early 20th-century blind poet and anarchist Vasyl/Vasilii Eroshenko (1890–1952), who lived and worked in Japan and China, came from the Ukrainian-Russian borderlands of Kursk gubernia. Japan still remembers the legendary Taihō Kōki/Ivan Boryshko (1940–2013), a sumo grand champion of the Shōwa era whose father Markiyan Boryshko was a Ukrainian living in Karafuto (Sakhalin). His grandson Yukio Naya now carries on that legacy in the sumo world.

Though often assumed to be Russian due to the imperial and Soviet contexts in which they lived, these figures emerge from Ukrainian soil and cultural memory. But what does that mean? Were they Ukrainian in the same way? Did they claim this identity? And how do we define it when identities were so often layered, overlapping, or even resisted?

The individuals featured in this book may not enjoy the global renown of Gogol or Korolyov, but their lives are no less extraordinary. Their "Ukrainianness" was often not a static identity, but one formed through movement, displacement, and choice. Ukraine, for them, was not only a birthplace, but a cultural horizon—a language, a memory, a vision of home. In writing about them, I am interested in Ukraine not just as a territory or nation-state, but as a network of imagined geographies and flexible identities.

In other words I claim that, in the minds of these protagonists, Ukraine emerges not as a fixed concept but as a layered and contested space: simultaneously a territory marked by shifting borders, a nation striving for political and sovereign coherence, and a cultural landscape shaped by diverse identities, languages, and historical traumas. These categories—territory, nation, culture—overlap and collide, each asserting itself differently depending on personal memory, ideology, and historical moment. The protagonists' varied perspectives do not resolve into a singular definition; rather, they reflect Ukraine's status as a site of ongoing negotiation between geography, identity, and imagination.

This project moves beyond the classic historical frameworks—whether the "ethnic" lens emphasised by Orest Subtelny[1] or the "territorial" approach advocated by Paul Robert Magocsi[2]—by considering diasporic life and transnational entanglement. I aim to present Ukraine as a shifting, interconnected space: not only defined by state borders, but by the movement of people, ideas, and affiliations across time.

As someone educated in Japan and deeply tied to its society, I initially wrote this book in Japanese to help Japanese readers understand Ukraine—its culture, people, and spirit—through real lives. But as this work now reaches an English-speaking audience, its purpose expands. What began as a celebration of Ukrainian figures abroad has become a meditation on displacement and survival.

The war in Ukraine is a vivid reminder of how frequently this land and its people have faced existential threats. And yet, over and over again, they have endured. This book tells the stories of individuals who were displaced, exiled, or forgotten—yet who turned hardship into strength and loss into legacy.

Even for those who were not ethnically Ukrainian, there is something profoundly Ukrainian in the landscapes, songs, embroidery, and unyielding sense of freedom that shaped these people. I hope this book offers a glimpse into the resilience of a nation and the lives of those who, though scarred by war and despite crossing borders, remain bound to their homeland in spirit and continue to fight with dignity and resilience.

This book brings to life the incredible journeys of border-crossers who embody the enduring spirit of Ukraine, offering a glimpse into their meaningful contributions to the world. Among them is Hryhorii Skovoroda, a philosopher whose concept of "srodna pratsya / kinship work" aligns with the Japanese idea of *tenshoku* [3]—a vocation sent by Heaven. Serhii Bort-

---

1 Orest Subtelny, *Ukraine: A History* (Toronto: University of Toronto Press, 1988).
2 Paul Robert Magocsi, *A History of Ukraine: The Land and Its Peoples* (Toronto: University of Toronto Press, 2010).
3 Tenshoku (天職) is a Japanese term meaning "heaven-sent job" or "calling." It refers to a vocation believed to be uniquely suited to a person's talents and

kevych/SergeiBortkiewicz, a composer from Kharkiv, turned the trials of war, emigration, and loss into music that radiates strength and lyricism. Ilya Mechnikov, a Nobel laureate and pioneer in immunology and gerontology, left behind groundbreaking discoveries that continue to resonate with generations of scientists.

Mykhailo Tereshchenko (Mikhail Tereschchenko in Russian), the last Ukrainian sugar tycoon, philanthropist, and financier, upheld the motto "Striving for the public good/benefit?," (referring to the Latin "pro bono publico" or "Стремлением к общественным пользам» in Russian) reflecting the nation's spirit of generosity. Sonia Delaunay, a visionary artist, captivated the world with her mastery of colour, design, and innovation. Igor Sikorsky (or Ihor Sikorsky in Ukrainian), a Kyiv-born aviation pioneer, overcame the upheavals of revolution and war to realise his dreams in the USA, becoming a symbol of resilience and ingenuity.

Sofia Yablonska (or Sophie Yabslonska-Oudin in French), a globetrotting writer and photographer, beautifully fused Ukrainian and Asian aesthetics in her work, leaving behind a legacy of cultural synthesis. Ivan Svit (Ivan Svetlanov in Russian, or John V. Sweet in English and イワン・スウィット in Japanese), a journalist and cultural bridge-builder, spent decades in Northeast Asia forging connections between Ukraine and Japan. Stepan Levynskyi (or Stefan Lewinski in Polish, Stephan Lewinsky in French or ステパン・レウィンスキ in Japanese), a diplomat, writer and cultural ambassador, exemplified the fusion of East and West, offering a unique perspective on global cooperation. Finally, Archduke Wilhelm of Austria, who embraced the name Vasyl Vyshyvanyi, adopted Ukraine as his homeland, demonstrating resilience and cultural integration in the most extraordinary way.

Throughout this book, I have chosen to use Ukrainian spellings for personal names and place names (e.g. *Kyiv*, *Odesa*, *Dnipro*) in keeping with current international standards and in recognition

---

character—work that one is naturally meant to do. Unlike a typical job, a *tenshoku* is seen as deeply fulfilling and spiritually aligned with one's life purpose, often carrying a sense of moral or existential destiny.

of Ukraine's present-day sovereignty and cultural revival. However, readers should be aware that in the late 19th and early 20th centuries—when individuals like Igor Sikorsky were active—Russian forms such as *Kiev, Odessa,* and *Yekaterinoslav* were more commonly used, both officially and colloquially, particularly among the educated elite and within imperial administrative contexts. Where historically relevant, I may note both versions (e.g. *Kyiv/Kiev*) or clarify the historical name in use at the time. This approach is not meant to impose modern identity retroactively, but rather to balance historical accuracy with the evolving understanding of national and cultural identities in Ukraine today. Readers should keep in mind that language, like identity, was fluid and contested in the period under discussion—and continues to be today.

Many individuals mentioned in this work were active in multilingual or diasporic contexts, and their names may appear in different forms depending on the language, alphabet, or transliteration system used. In cases where a person used multiple names—such as "Ivan Svit" in Ukrainian and "John V. Sweet" in English—I have selected the form most associated with the context in which they are discussed, or the name they themselves most consistently used. Variants are noted where relevant. This approach acknowledges the fluidity of identity and language across regions, histories, and sources.

Each of these individuals faced immense challenges, yet they pursued their dreams with determination, leaving an indelible mark on the world. Their stories are a testament to Ukrainian resilience and offer valuable lessons in adaptability, strength, and vision.

Among the individuals featured are nine figures born in regions such as Kyiv, Kharkiv, Lviv, Odesa, and Poltava—alongside one remarkable outsider, Archduke Wilhelm of Austria (1895–1948), who embraced a Ukrainian identity under the name Vasyl Vyshyvanyi and shared Ukraine's fate as a victim of Soviet repression. Together, their stories transcend borders—physical, mental, and cultural—and reveal how vision and perseverance can shape the world.

Although this book features ten individuals, the title "Nine Life Journeys" reflects the overarching narrative focus—nine distinct paths through which Ukraine's historical experience is explored. One chapter, dedicated to Archduke Wilhelm of Austria (Vasyl Vyshyvanyi), stands somewhat apart as a symbolic, adopted Ukrainian life—exceptional in origin but deeply tied to Ukraine's fate.

The final chapter of this book turns to borders themselves—not only as geopolitical lines, but as symbolic thresholds that have long haunted, challenged, and inspired Ukrainians. Throughout their history, borders have been both prison and passage: barriers of war and loss, but also zones of exchange, creativity, and survival. This ambiguity—both constraint and opportunity—is key to understanding Ukraine's complex past and present.

This book is not simply about famous lives. It is also a portrait of Ukraine—its culture, its endurance, its openness. It is about resilience, love of music and nature, creativity, multilingualism, and the power of art and memory. It is an effort to shine a light on the contributions of individuals whose stories deserve a wider stage.

This book was welcomed in Japan, and I am very happy to now present this rewritten and expanded text to the anglophone world. I hope it will foster deeper understanding and stronger support for Ukraine, and that you will enjoy the reading and find inspiration in the lives of these brave people.

Olga Khomenko
Oxford, August 2025

Acknowledgment

I would like to express my deepest gratitude to all those who supported me throughout the completion of this project.

First and foremost, I am sincerely thankful to Professor Serhii Plokhii for his brilliant mentorship and invaluable friendship. I also wish to thank Professor Andreas Umland for encouraging the idea of publishing this work in English. My heartfelt appreciation goes to Professor Zbigniew Wojnowski, who not only contributed a brilliant introduction to this book but has also been a great source of support over the past three years.

I am deeply grateful to the Council for At-Risk Academics, British Academy, Professor Paul Chaisty and Professor Sho Konishi for their mentorship, unwavering support, and for providing a safe and welcoming environment at Oxford, allowing me to continue my studies during the time of war. Thank you also go to Professor Roy Alister for the meaningful conversations and insightful advice. I am grateful to Professor Diego Sánchez-Ancochea for his support.

To my dear friend Marcel Garbos — thank you for your kindness, friendship, and support, and for reading the manuscript and offering thoughtful feedback. I am also grateful to Sherzod Muminov and Will Medd for encouraging me to publish this work in English.

I owe a special thanks to Alina Kudina, who helped me translate the manuscript from Japanese into English, and to my editor, Sally Spode, whose guidance helped me refine my voice.

I also would like to thank to Professor Hidehiko Sekizawa for his brilliant mentorship over several decades. A very special thank you goes to Professor Kazuo Nakai, who introduced me to the world of Japanese academia and the Ukrainian diaspora in Asia.

I am wholeheartedly thankful to Ashley Woods and Wendy Ko, and to their children Maya and Tyler, I am deeply grateful for giving me a home in the UK, for your thoughtful "parenting advice," and for all the wonderful times we shared together. I am also grateful to Martha and Kevin Grieve for their friendship, fabulous sense of humour, and for letting me stay in their home when it was too late to return to Oxford.

I would like to thank Professor Serge Cipko for his generous support of my research on Ivan Svit and the Ukrainian diaspora in the Far East and Asia. I am also deeply grateful to Natalya Khanenko-Friesen for her encouragement of my work.

My heartfelt thanks go to the family of the late Nicolas Melnyk, whose stories about Ukrainians in China enriched my understanding of the diaspora. I deeply appreciate the help and support for my archival research from Larysa Zanyk, Professor Albert Kipa, Dr. Tamara Skrypka, and the Ukrainian Academy of Arts and Sciences in the USA (UVAN). I am also very thankful to Olha Aleksych for her invaluable assistance with the archives at Harvard University.

Also my sincere thanks to Matt Watts for taking me to the National Gallery of Australia in Canberra back in 2017. Special gratitude goes to William Mitchel Reed for reading the very first version of this text and providing his valuable comments. I also very much appreciate Evgen Yashchuk for the inspiring conversations and his support and friendship.

A genuine thank you to Arthur McFarlane for his suggestions, comments, friendship, steady presence, and wonderful sense of humour.

I wish to express my earnest gratitude to Mayotte Magnus-Lewińska for her generous and thoughtful support of my research on her father-in-law, Stepan Levynskyi/Lewinski. His legacy, and the insights she shared, greatly deepened my understanding and helped bring this project to life. I am equally indebted to the Foundation of Sofia Yablonska and the president Veronika Homeniuk as well as for the granddaughter of Sofia, Natalie Yablonska-Ouden, whose gracious assistance in providing rare archival materials and photographs of Sofia as well as her close friend Stepan Levynskyy proved invaluable. Their generosity, trust, and encouragement have meant more to me than words can fully convey.

I would also like to thank all my colleagues and friends who supported me over the past three difficult years of war and helped keep me going: Professor Roger Goodman, Dr. Martina Baradel, Dr. Michael Rochlitz, Dr. Juliana Buriticá Alzate, Dr. Chinami Oka, Dr. Alice Baldock and Dr. Marius Palz and Mihoko Nari from University of Oxford, as well as my dearest Ukrainian friends Olena Vovk, Serhii Lokot, Oksana and Aleksey Kondratjev, Oksana and Oleg Kirichek, Mariana Motrunych, Sasha Petrauskaite, and Mariam Kunchulia. I also deeply appreciated the kindness and support of Junko Imanishi and Atsumi International Foundation.

I am also thankful to Sugimoto Satoshi for his support of Ukraine and unwavering dedication to learning the Ukrainian language, which has been truly inspiring. Finally, I would like to extend a very special thank you to Keiichiro Kawakami and his wonderful family. Their warm welcome and hospitality in London always provided me with comfort, joy, and unforgettable moments.

A special thank you goes to Yuliia Krylova, my former student and a brilliant designer, who created the inspiring cover of this book using an image by Robert Delaunay. You may wonder why it is not a Sonia Delaunay picture on the cover—but in this choice, I also wanted to acknowledge the significant others behind the public figures featured in this book. Without them—without family and friends—it would have been even harder for these individuals to endure the challenges they faced.

A special gratitude goes to my Japanese "mom," A.Y.—she preferred to be known by this acronym—who unfortunately passed away in December 2022. Her courage, generosity, and example of how to live bravely continue to inspire me. I will never forget her.

Lastly, I wish to express my deepest gratitude to my family, and especially to my mother, who continues to be a source of strength and inspiration.

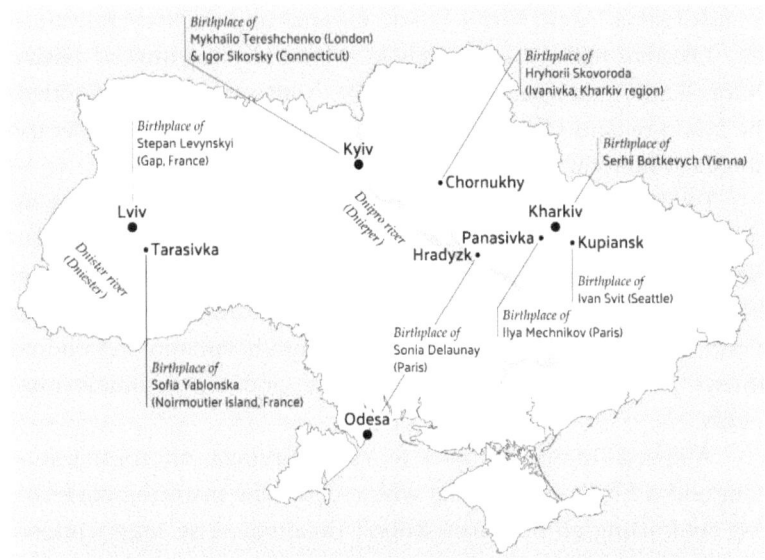

Birthplaces and death places of the protagonists

*There are two theories on the place of birth of Sonia Delaunay.

An Itinerant Freethinker
Hryhorii Skovoroda
(03.12.1722-09.11.1794)

In Kontraktova Square, in Kyiv, stands a bronze statue of Hryhorii Skovoroda[4]. A philosopher, musician, and teacher, Skovoroda was a brilliant man of many talents who lived in the 18th-century. He entered the Kyiv-Mohyla Academy at the age of 16, and today his statue, created in 1977, stands looking at his alma mater. The students of what is now the National University of Kyiv-Mohyla Academy clean the bronze statue during the academy's annual festival on October 15th, and for June's graduation ceremony they clothe it with a cap and gown. There is a superstition among the students that if you rub Skovoroda's shoes, you will get a good grade on your exam. The 90-year-old sculptor Ivan Kavaleridze had originally planned to portray Skovoroda barefoot with a Bible in his hand and a crucifix around his neck, but in the face of religious persecution by the Soviet government, he was forced to give up this design. As a result, he portrayed Skovoroda with a cloth bag in his right hand and shoes on his feet.

There are other statues of Skovoroda in Kyiv, and his portrait, along with a picture of a fountain representing his philosophy, appears on the 500-hryvnia bill, which used to be the highest denomination in Ukraine until inflation in recent years created the need for a 1,000-hryvnia bill. Whenever I use a 500-hryvnia bill, I am struck by its resemblance to the Japanese 10,000-yen bill that features the educator, philosopher, and reformer Fukuzawa Yukichi[5], and I cannot help but feel that the two men had much in common.

---

4 Unless otherwise specified, all dates are expressed in the Gregorian calendar.
5 Fukuzawa Yukichi (1835–1901) was a pivotal figure in shaping the ideological foundation of the Meiji state, not through formal political power, but as a philosopher of modernity and national transformation. A firm advocate of Western learning, individual autonomy, and rational thought, Fukuzawa

Skovoroda was born in 1722 in the village of Chornukhy in what the Poltava Oblast of central Ukraine is now. Fukuzawa was born in Osaka in 1835, almost a century later, to a low-ranking samurai family from the Nakatsu domain in Kyushu. Following the early death of his father, his family moved back to their former home, so Fukuzawa, like Skovoroda, was raised in the countryside.

Григор. о͞с Σ.

From a young age, Skovoroda enjoyed learning and was recognised for his talent in music and singing. He moved to Kyiv[6] at the age of 16 and studied at the Mohyla Academy but left after three years to join the private choir of Empress Elizabeth (Elizaveta) of Russia (1709-1762), the daughter of Tsar Peter the Great, in Moscow and St. Petersburg. Empress Elizabeth had a soft spot for men with beautiful voices and gathered them from all over the country.

Skovoroda immersed himself in the study of French and Italian at the Russian imperial court. He received a good salary, and his parents were exempt from paying taxes. Oleksiy Rozum

---

helped redefine Japan's national identity in the late 19th-century. Through his writings — especially *An Encouragement of Learning* and *An Outline of a Theory of Civilization* — he promoted the idea that Japan must embrace science, education, and social reform to resist Western domination and become a "civilized" nation on equal footing with the West. He rejected Confucian hierarchy and argued for a meritocratic society grounded in practical knowledge. Though he distanced himself from government roles, his ideas deeply influenced Meiji leaders in areas such as education, law, and civic morality. He also founded private Keio University in Tokyo, still one of the most famous in Japan.

6   Skovoroda spent part of his life in Kyiv, which was at the time an important centre of Orthodox learning within the Russian Empire, often referred to as 'Kiev' in Western accounts.

(Alexei Razumovsky in Russian) (1709–1771), a senior Ukrainian member of the same choir, rose up to become a count and married Empress Elizabeth in a secret wedding ceremony. Unlike Razumovsky, Skovoroda had no interest in becoming a political figure, and after three years, he grew tired of serving at the palace and returned to the Mohyla Academy. Another three years later, he was recruited to the Tokaj Commission for the procurement of wines for the tsar's court, which resulted in him spending the next five years travelling around Hungary, Italy, Germany, and Austria. This enabled him to witness foreign cultures and lifestyles with his own eyes, and he later incorporated his experiences into his philosophical theories.

Similarly, Fukuzawa had a thirst for learning and became fluent in the Dutch language after moving at the age of 19 to Nagasaki and the following year to Osaka. After moving to Edo (present-day Tokyo), where he founded a Dutch-language school, he was chosen to take part in government missions to the United States and Europe to acquire Western knowledge. Like Skovoroda, he was able to experience foreign societies firsthand and later wrote *An Outline of a Theory of Civilization* (1875) about their politics and culture.

At the age of 28, Skovoroda returned to Ukraine, a Cossack Hetmanate, which was soon to be dismantled by Catherine II but still existed officially, although he could not establish his own school, he taught at the Kyiv-Mohyla Academy. The freedom to act and speak according to his personal priorities and beliefs was of the utmost importance to him, leading him to decline a government post as philosopher at the imperial court. Likewise, Fukuzawa did not accept any government positions and remained a private citizen throughout his life. Fukuzawa was, however, able to exert significant influence through his publications, including a newspaper called Jijishinpō (Current Events), which called for the adoption of Western learning to enable Japan to modernise, whereas Skovoroda's works remained unpublished in his lifetime.

Skovoroda was so outspoken that he was expelled from the Academy, but instead of conforming to societal rules, he chose to live a life of spiritual freedom. He travelled throughout Ukraine for the last 30 years of his life, spreading his ideas as an itinerant philosopher with little more than a Bible and a flute. Such a lifestyle was highly unusual in 18th-century Ukraine, where mobility was limited and often tightly controlled. Some scholars speculate that he may have been inspired by the example of clergymen who wandered in search of teaching posts before eventually settling. But unlike them, Skovoroda never settled. His way of life also evokes the figure of the kobzar—the blind, wandering minstrel of Ukrainian tradition—well known to readers of Shevchenko's poetry, who moved from village to village sharing songs, stories, and moral teachings. Like the kobzars, Skovoroda lived outside formal institutions, relying on oral wisdom, memory, and personal charisma rather than official authority.

Tall and elegant, he dressed like a clergyman and lived the life of a stoic. It is said that he slept four hours a day, rose before sunrise, and ate only one meal a day. In this he was akin to a Japanese Buddhist mendicant monk, but whereas they would return to their temples to chant their prayers, Skovoroda walked across Ukraine talking to people and telling them what he had seen, read, and thought. Even though newspapers in imperial Russia began to be published in 1703, peasants remained illiterate and did not have money to buy newspapers, so news and knowledge were spread by word of mouth. Skovoroda spoke the local Ukrainian language and could communicate with them well.

Hryhorii Skovoroda wrote primarily in a blend of early modern Ukrainian, Church Slavonic, and Latin, occasionally using Russian, reflecting the multilingual scholarly tradition of 18th-century Eastern Europe. This linguistic range indicates his ability to move between different cultural spheres—vernacular and elite, borderland and metropolitan—as was characteristic of intellectuals in multilingual and imperial contexts.

Skovoroda's writings, although well preserved, were not published until 200 years after his death. We are now able to read *The Complete Works of Skovoroda* in two volumes, which includes poems, philosophical allegories, dialogues, letters to his students and close friends, and songs. We still cherish his ideas and his unique worldview with its central concept of

"Srodna pratsia" — a key concept in Skovoroda's philosophy, often rendered as "congenial labour" or "natural vocation", meaning work that aligns with one's true nature. He believed that everybody has particular talents and that they should do work that makes use of them; in his words, "If you do not consider your work satisfying and pleasurable, you will not gain from it." His philosophy was that true peace, and joy can be found in doing the work that one loves and this is the way to maintain a harmonious relationship with God; and when people have peace and joy in their hearts, the nation will prosper. Writing before the rise of Romantic nationalism — and Ukrainian ethnic nationalism in particular — he did not classify people by social rank or language, but by their capacity to seek truth, live according to conscience, and remain in harmony with their "inner self". For Skovoroda, this constituted the "true people" who believed in the importance of treating others with kindness, he made friends wherever he went and developed a strong sense of morality. His emphasis on the individual has something in common with Fukuzawa in the early Meiji period, who stressed the importance of personal virtue and spiritual well-being as the basis for building a prosperous Japanese nation. It is also interesting to note that the modern-day Japanese concept of ikigai (meaning "a passion that gives value and joy to life") has many similarities with Skovoroda's notion of "work that pleases the heart."

On the 500-hryvnia bill, water from the fountain flows into vessels of different shapes and sizes. According to Skovoroda, this represents the ideal society in which everyone's differences are valued. The text says: "Equality is harmony, not uniformity."

Skovoroda also believed that it does not require great effort to obtain what you really need and that if you must force yourself to do something, then maybe you don't truly need it. This is similar to the idea of "flow"[7] proposed by the modern Hungarian

---

7   The concept of a highly focused mental state conducive to productivity, in which a person is fully immersed in a sense of energised focus, full involvement, and enjoyment in performing an activity. In essence, flow is

American psychologist Mihaly Csikszentmihalyi. According to Skovoroda, human happiness consists of a small number of things, and God gives us everything we need. However, there was also a place in his philosophy for "a piece of luxury in daily life." Although he lived the life of an ascetic, it is said that the flute he carried in his cloth bag had an ivory head and that he loved good wine, Parmesan cheese, and cigarettes. In another parallel between the men, Fukuzawa also had a penchant for rare and beautiful foreign things: he was the first to bring a leather notebook to Japan and he liked cigarettes, which were often scattered around his room.

Skovoroda's understanding of "srodna pratsia" — work aligned with one's nature — reflects his belief that each child is born with unique, inherent abilities that education should nurture rather than suppress. Skovoroda believed that "everyone should know about the people and also know about themselves among them." He never bowed his head, even before noblemen and emperors. He did not bow even when he stood before Tsarina Catharine the Great. When she was angered by this, he said to her: "You wanted to see me. However, if I bow, my face will look down and you won't be able to see me as you wished." When asked to work at the palace, he replied: "I will never leave Ukraine. For me, sheep and a flute are more important than a royal crown."

As well as the flute, Skovoroda could also play the violin, bandura, and harp, and he believed that poetry and music were both important elements in his philosophy. In Japan, for example, texts with musical notation have been passed down from as long ago as the Heian period[8], but sadly there has been no such tradition in Ukraine. In the 18th-century, no one recorded Skovoroda's music. However, there is a letter in the National Library of

---

characterised by complete absorption in what one does and the resulting transformation in one's sense of time.

8   The Heian period (794–1185 CE) is a classical era in Japanese history, known for its courtly culture, refinement, and the flourishing of literature, art, and aesthetics. It was named after the capital city Heian-kyō (modern-day Kyoto), which became the centre of imperial rule and aristocratic life.

Ukraine, likely written by Skovoroda himself, which contains a score for his song Cherubic Hymn. There are also Ukrainian folk songs and music that are known as Skovorodynski psalms, and Valentin Silvestrov, a Ukrainian composer of contemporary music, has set Skovoroda's poem *The Garden of Divine Songs* to music.

Hryhorii Skovoroda was born and lived in what is now central Ukraine, deeply immersed in the country's cultural and intellectual traditions. His life was closely tied to Ukrainian regions such as Kyiv and Kharkiv, and he belonged to the Cossack-humanist intelligentsia shaped by the Kyiv-Mohyla Academy. Though he wrote in Church Slavonic, Latin, and early literary Ukrainian, his style, imagery, and worldview were distinctly Ukrainian, drawing heavily on folklore and proverbs. His philosophy — rooted in freedom, self-knowledge, and inner harmony — reflected the Ukrainian spirit of independence and contrasted sharply with the Russian imperial ideal of obedience to authority. Today, he is honoured as a national philosopher of Ukraine, while in Russia he remains a more distant, academic figure.

Skovoroda was a genius of his time who did not care about social norms and made his own rules for living. His humanistic ideas about how to live, work, and improve oneself outside of the confines of 18th-century society still resonate with people today. It seems that he even died according to his own fashion. It is said that Skovoroda, having reached the age of 71, knew the day he was going to die, and on that day, he dug his own grave and lay down in it to breathe his last. In his will he requested that these words should be written on his gravestone: "The world tried to catch me, but it failed."

Ilya Mechnikov
A Founding Figure in Immunology and Gerontology
(15.05.1845-15.07.1916)

May 15th is Yoghurt Day in Japan. It was proposed by Meiji Co., Ltd[9] in 2012, also on that day is the birthday of Ilya Mechnikov, a Ukrainian-born biologist, who discovered the beneficial effects of yoghurt's lactic acid bacteria on the human body.

Ilya's elder brother Lev (sometimes called Leo) travelled to Switzerland, Italy and Japan, introducing the ideas of anarchism to Japan after the Meiji Restoration of 1868[10]. Also, he established the first Russian language course in Japan. It is probably not widely recognised that the two brothers, born in Ukraine before the invention of the aeroplane, had a great influence on Japan in terms of both ideology and health.

---

9   Meiji Co., Ltd. (Meiji Company, Limited) is a major Japanese food and pharmaceutical company best known internationally for its dairy products (including yoghurt), confectionery, and health-related foods, as well as its work in nutritional science and probiotics. The company also has a pharmaceutical division that focuses on infectious diseases, vaccines, and wellness.

10 The Meiji Restoration was a pivotal political and social transformation in Japan that marked the end of over two centuries of Tokugawa shogunate rule and the formal restoration of imperial power under Emperor Meiji. Beginning in 1868, this movement ushered in rapid modernisation, centralisation of the state, and the adoption of Western political, military, and industrial systems. It laid the foundation for Japan's emergence as a modern nation-state and a major world power in the decades that followed. While much of the new knowledge came from Europe and America, the Russian Empire also played a role in transmitting scientific and intellectual ideas to Japan. For an in-depth study of Meiji Japan's intellectual formation and the significant role of Russian influence alongside European and American ideas, see Sho Konishi's *Anarchist Modernity: Cooperatism and Japanese-Russian Intellectual Relations in Modern Japan*, Harvard East Asian Monographs 356 (Cambridge, MA: Harvard University Press, 2013) and the later volume by Olga V. Solovieva and Sho Konishi, *Japan's Russia: Challenging the East-West Paradigm* (Cambria Press 2021).

Ilya Mechnikov (known in French as Élie Metchnikoff) was born in 1845 in the village of Panasivka in the Kharkiv region, part of the Russian Empire back then. He was the youngest of five children of a landowning aristocratic family and was given the same name as his father. His father, a military officer with a taste for extravagance, married the daughter of a wealthy Polish-Jewish financial official. His mother, Emilia Nevakhovich, came from a cultured and intellectually active Jewish family; her father, Lev Nevakhovich, was a writer, translator, and prominent figure in the Jewish Enlightenment (Haskalah) movement in the Russian Empire. After squandering his wife's inheritance, Mechnikov's father moved the family to a rural estate to lead a quiet life (although some say it was Ivanivka village, not Panasivka village in the beginning, and this has never been settled). Panasivka village was settled after the Zaporizhzhian Sich (a Cossack stronghold) was destroyed by Empress Catherine II. Mechnikov's father loved to drink and play cards and his mother was kind and loved music and literature. His maternal grandfather was fond of culture and literature, and was close to many intellectuals of the time, such as poets Aleksandr Pushkin (1799-1837) and Ivan Krylov (1769-1844). Of all the children—one girl and four boys—none of them followed the military path of their father. Ivan became a judge; Lev, a geographer and anarchist; Mykola, a government official; and Ilya, who had no interest in politics, became a biologist. Their only daughter, Kateryna, was happily married and left the family home.

Ilya, the youngest, was small and restless, with light brown hair. He was called Mercury at home because he was small and always running around. His mother Emilia, who oversaw all the children's affairs, had the ability to recognise the talents of each child. Ilya, who was educated at home, was most interested in different flowers and insects. He loved to watch them, observe changes, and draw them. The music played by his mother on their piano was another great love. His dual interests in biology and music, developing later into a particular taste for opera, remained with him throughout his long life.

From the age of seven he had been collecting and preserving flowers and herbs as specimens under the supervision of a private tutor, like a real scholar. He was the smallest one, so often his siblings did not pay much attention to him: and he wanted attention. So, sometimes he organised "lectures" and paid his siblings with pocket money he gained from parents so that they would listen to him.

The youngest of five children, he realised from a young age that studying was the only way for him to gain attention, independence, and to assert control. Moreover, was very much focused on his studies. Usually, he did not do anything that did not serve his purpose; he divided his studies into subjects that required study and those that did not. He was very particular.

Ivan and Lev entered private school in St. Petersburg, while Mykola and Kateryna went to high school and college in Kharkiv, and Ilya attended a local high school. Ilya also read a lot. He read a lot of European philosophers' writings, especially on materialism. In school, he chose to study German, because he learned French at home. After graduating from high school in 1862 with all As, he decided to study at the University of Würzburg in the German state of Bavaria. Founded in 1402, it is one of the oldest universities which has produced many famous scholars of medicine like Carl Caspar von Siebold (1736–1807), a pioneer of modern surgical practice and founder of one of the first operating rooms and Alois Alzheimer (1864–1915), a psychiatrist, and neuropathologist best known for identifying the first published case of what would later be named Alzheimer's disease.

Ilya, who was 17 years old at the time, went to Bavaria in the middle of summer and had to wait a month and a half for admission. Even though he spoke good German, he did not make any friends during that first summer in Germany. It was his first time living abroad alone. He was waiting for school to start and felt very lonely in Bavaria. He ended up not managing to wait and returned to his parents' house.

Upon his return to Ukraine, Ilya enrolled in the Faculty of Physics and Mathematics at Kharkiv University, very close by. Initially he wanted to enter medical school, but apparently accepted his mother's advice. Thinking him too delicate to face illness and pain, she encouraged him towards the structured, rational world of physics and mathematics—a realm governed by clarity and logic, not blood and chaos. At the same time, he became fascinated by Darwin's theory of natural selection.

When he entered university, he was very eager to study and very quickly completed a four year course within two years. Raised with religious teachings at home, he later committed himself to Darwinism and seems to have lost his faith in God. In 1864, after graduating from the university, he obtained a research position at the laboratory of the famous German biologist of the time Rudolf Leuckart (1822–1898) in the region of Hessen. Mechnikov went to the University of Giessen in Hessen in the autumn and worked there until March of the following year. Thereafter, he stayed with his brother Lev in Geneva in neighbouring Switzerland for a while, where he met Russian political thinker Alexander Herzen (1812–1870) and the anarchist Mikhail Bakunin (1814–1876), and others from his older brother's close circle. Yet, once again, surrounded by revolutionary thinkers and activists, Ilya realised that he had no real interest in political engagement.

In the summer of 1865, he was invited to Italy by famous Russian zoologist and a pioneering embryologist and one of the founders of comparative and evolutionary embryology Alexander Kovalevsky (1840–1901), who was only five years older and lived in Italian Naples. Kovalevsky was conducting research on the embryonic development of both vertebrates and invertebrates.

During this time Mechikov also became acquainted with the famous Russian physiologist Ivan Sechenov (1829–1905) often called the "father of Russian physiology", known for his work on the central nervous system and reflexes and the Russian surgeon and pioneer of field medicine doctor Nikolai Pirogov (1810–1881). Both men were spending their summer vacation in Italy, and they were deeply impressed by the young scholar Ilya Mechnikov. In 1867, not yet 22 years old, he was awarded a master's degree without examination by the University of St. Petersburg in recognition of his earlier research.

In the winter of 1869, he caught a cold and stayed at his friend Andrei Beketov's house. Beketov's niece, Lyudmila Fedorovich, took care of him. This was the beginning of a relationship which would lead to marriage. Unfortunately, Lyudmila contracted tuberculosis and had to go to Italy, where the climate was much better than in St. Petersburg, for rehabilitation. Ilya needed money to pay for his wife's treatment, so he gave lectures and translated academic papers when he could. While continuing his embryological research, Mechnikov contributed to the understanding of germ layer formation and supported the idea of a common origin of multicellular animals through the gastrula stage, helping clarify phylogenetic relationships among major animal groups. In 1870, he earned a doctorate in zoology. Since there was no cure for tuberculosis at the time, they moved from place to place in search of a better climate and living conditions: first to Germany, then to Switzerland, and finally to Madeira Island in Portugal—where, unfortunately, on April 20th, 1873, his wife Lyudmila passed away.

On his way back from his wife's funeral, Ilya stopped to visit his brother Lev in Switzerland, where, overwhelmed by grief, he attempted to take his own life with a morphine injection. However, his weakened body rejected the morphine, vomiting it all up. When he regained consciousness, he was determined to finish what he had started. He took a hot bath, followed by a cold shower, and went outside, hoping the shock would make him ill and bring about death. But as he walked, his attention was suddenly caught by insects circling a lamppost. Fascinated, he became so absorbed in observing them that he forgot his earlier intention to end his life.

Before reaching his 30s, Ilya's deteriorating eyesight led him to shift his focus from embryology to anthropology. Between 1872 and 1874, he conducted fieldwork in the steppe regions of Astrakhan and Stavropol, where he studied the indigenous Kalmyk people of Mongolian descent. He became particularly interested in their dietary practices, including their regular consumption of fermented dairy products such as yoghurt. This early exposure to traditional diets rich in lactic acid bacteria would later resurface in his scientific work on gut health and longevity. Mechnikov found that the comparative methods he had developed in embryology could also be effectively applied to anthropological research, laying the groundwork for his later studies on the role of intestinal flora in aging and immunity.

When Mechnikov returned to St. Petersburg in 1874 to resume his scientific work, his eyesight again began to deteriorate. On medical advice, he took a break from research and worked temporarily as a schoolteacher. During this time, he met Olga Belokopytova, a student of 15 years old, with whom he formed a close bond. Despite her young age, he proposed marriage, and she would later become his lifelong partner, intellectual companion, and biographer.

Despite her father's objections, Olga and Ilya married in February 1875, with the understanding that Ilya would take responsibility for her education. Olga became a certified teacher two years later, though she never pursued a teaching career. Over the course of their 30 year marriage, she supported Mechnikov as his partner, friend, student, and assistant. After his death, she honoured his legacy by publishing a biography of his life and work.

The spring of 1881 was marked by the assassination of Emperor Alexander II of Russia and a period of personal crisis for Mechnikov, who was then teaching at the University of Odesa/Odessa. During this time, his wife contracted epidemic typhus, and his deteriorating eyesight added to his distress. Believing he might also be infected with an incurable disease, he attempted suicide for the second time—this time by injecting himself with the typhus pathogen in an act of self-experimentation. He developed a serious infection but ultimately recovered, and, somewhat surprisingly, found that his eyesight had improved. Meanwhile, political unrest erupted at the university, and Mechnikov, partly due to his association with his well-known anarchist brother Lev, was suspected of involvement. Under pressure, he resigned from his position at Odesa/Odessa.

Around the same time, Olga's father, Nikolai, died in an accident, and Ilya's family inherited several properties, including farmland in the Kyiv and Chernihiv regions. Although Mechnikov took on the responsibility of caring for Olga's seven younger siblings, the inheritance was substantial enough to relieve the family of financial concerns. At one of the farms, he began applying scientific methods to practical problems — experimenting with ways to protect beets and wheat from insect pests. These efforts reflected his belief that science could be used not only to understand nature but also to improve daily life through rational, evidence-based solutions. However, despite his efforts, the agricultural experiments did not lead to the success he had hoped for.

In the autumn of 1882, while staying on the Italian coast with his wife, Mechnikov observed how a starfish's body responded to the insertion of a rose thorn. This simple yet striking observation inspired him to develop a theory of the immune system based on the idea that certain cells in the body react to foreign intrusions. Soon afterward, he presented his findings at the Congress of Natural History and Medical Sciences in Odesa/Odessa, introducing terms such as *phagocytes* and *macrophages* (a type of white blood cell with phagocytic properties). However, his ideas were poorly received by many in the medical community, who were unfamiliar with his terminology and sceptical of his zoological approach to human physiology. At the time, interdisciplinary thinking was not widely accepted, and drawing parallels between humans and lower animals was seen as controversial, if not heretical.

Between 1882 and 1886, Mechnikov had no formal affiliation with a research institution and spent much of his time travelling abroad while continuing his scientific work independently. In 1886, he was appointed director of the newly established Bacteriological Station in Odesa/Odessa, which was modelled on Louis Pasteur's pioneering work in Paris, particularly in vaccine development for infectious diseases. The station began testing vaccines on livestock, but some of the experiments — carried out by researchers under Mechnikov's supervision — led to the deaths of numerous animals. The incident sparked public criticism and professional backlash, especially from veterinary authorities. Although Mechnikov was not personally charged, the controversy damaged his standing and made it increasingly difficult to continue his work in Russia. He briefly considered moving to Germany, but faced resistance from German scientists who remained sceptical of his phagocyte theory. In 1887, he accepted an invitation from Louis Pasteur and joined the newly founded Pasteur Institute in Paris, where he found a more supportive scientific environment.

Mechnikov spent the final 28 years of his life in France, working at the Pasteur Institute. After the death of Louis Pasteur in 1895, he became the institute's deputy director and emerged as one of the leading figures in early immunology. His discovery of phagocytosis laid the groundwork for the theory of cellular immunity and helped define how the immune system detects and responds to foreign invaders. While not an illustrator by profession, he produced detailed cellular drawings that reflected a sophisticated understanding of immune responses. His experimental work with infectious diseases and vaccines contributed to the broader foundation upon which the field of immunopathology would later be built.

The now-common expression "the body is fighting infections" can be traced back to Mechnikov's pioneering ideas about the immune system. Until October 1908, when he was awarded the Nobel Prize in Physiology or Medicine for his theory of cellular immunity, his work was met with scepticism by many in the scientific community. The Nobel Prize brought renewed attention to his research, significantly elevated his reputation, and earned him international recognition. In keeping with his scholarly commitments, Mechnikov declined to attend the award ceremony in Stockholm, as it conflicted with his lecture schedule at the Pasteur

Institute. However, he promised to deliver a lecture in Stockholm the following summer, and in 1909, he fulfilled that promise by presenting a lecture in French on the immune system.

Building on his earlier research on animal cells and immune function, in his later years Ilya Mechnikov turned his attention to the study of aging and longevity. He became a pioneer in two emerging fields: gerontology, the scientific study of aging, and thanatology, the study of death. In fact, Mechnikov coined the term *gerontology* in 1903. He proposed that aging was not simply the result of cells wearing out simultaneously, but rather that certain aging cells may attack and damage still-functioning ones — a concept rooted in his understanding of immune and cellular behaviour. While travelling in Bulgaria, he was struck by the remarkable number of healthy elderly people and noted that some individuals lived close to a hundred years. Upon investigation, he attributed this longevity to the regular consumption of fermented milk products — particularly yoghurt rich in lactic acid bacteria. This observation not only reinforced his theories on the gut microbiome and health, but also helped popularise Bulgarian yoghurt internationally as a health food.

When looking at photographs of the young Ilya Mechnikov, one might notice a certain loneliness in his eyes. As he grew older, however, he became increasingly reflective and philosophically grounded. In 1908, he published a book titled *Études sur la nature humaine: Essai de philosophie optimiste* (Studies on Human Nature: An Essay in Optimistic Philosophy), first in French and later in Russian. In this work, Mechnikov explored themes of pessimism and optimism, drawing on Greek and Roman thought as well as the works of writers such as Alexander Pushkin (1799–1837), Mikhail Lermontov (1814–1841), and Johann Wolfgang von Goethe (1749–1832). Interwoven with reflections on plant and animal biology and the science of human aging, the book also delves into his own youthful struggles and the broader phenomenon of artistic despair and suicide. Today, the book remains compelling not only for its scientific insights but also for its moral and philosophical depth.

Mechnikov died of heart disease in 1916 in Paris, at a time when the research environment had become increasingly difficult due to the outbreak of World War I. His death marked a profound loss for global science. At the turn of the 20th-century, Mechnikov had made major contributions across multiple disciplines—interacting with scholars around the world and applying comparative methods drawn from biology, zoology, and medicine. His work on human aging mobilised all his scientific knowledge and embodied his belief in the unity of life sciences.

A complex and determined figure, Mechnikov was the youngest child in his family, often solitary, and at times deeply troubled—he attempted suicide twice and faced sharp criticism from fellow scientists throughout his career. It took him years to find stability in his personal life, yet his deep curiosity remained constant. That curiosity was the source of his energy and originality. Born on Ukrainian land, a citizen of the Russian Empire, and of Jewish descent, Mechnikov defied academic boundaries. Though trained as a zoologist, he boldly crossed into medicine, even as many resisted his interdisciplinary approach.

Ilya Mechnikov was born in 1845 in what is now the Kharkiv region of Ukraine, to a Ukrainian-Jewish mother and a Russian army officer father. Though his family spoke Russian, they lived in a Ukrainian cultural environment and maintained close ties with the local population. Educated at Kharkiv University, Mechnikov's early scientific formation took place in a setting that was Ukrainian in both geography and spirit. He wrote primarily in Russian and French and pursued a cosmopolitan scientific career in Saint Petersburg, Odesa/Odessa, and Paris. Like many intellectuals of the 19th-century Russian Empire, he did not define himself by nationality, but his background fits a common pattern born in a multiethnic empire, educated across regions, and shaped by international ideals. While not part of the Ukrainian national movement, his early life was deeply rooted in Ukrainian soil, and today he is recognised as part of Ukraine's scientific legacy—alongside his contributions to French and Russian thought.

Today, as the world continues to confront emerging diseases, Mechnikov's life reminds us of the importance of nurturing environments where independent and unconventional thinkers can thrive. His legacy is not only in the discoveries he made but in the spirit of fearless inquiry he embodied—an enduring example of how curiosity can shape the course of science.

The Last Romantic in Exile
Serhii Bortkevych/Sergei Bortkiewicz
(1877-1952)

Ukraine is blessed with a rich and vibrant musical heritage that spans centuries and borders. In the 18th-century, the country produced some of Eastern Europe's most important Baroque composers, including Dmytro Bortniansky (1751-1825), Maksym Berezovsky (1745-1777), and Artemiy Vedel (1767-1808). These composers blended Ukrainian liturgical and folk traditions with Western European classical forms, leaving a lasting imprint on sacred music and choral traditions. One of Ukraine's most iconic contributions to world music is the folk song *Shchedryk,* a traditional New Year's carol. In the early 20th - century, composer Mykola Leontovych (1877-1921) transformed it into a choral masterpiece, which later  became internationally famous as *Carol of the Bells*. Its haunting melody and rhythmic structure have made it one of the most recognisable Christmas songs worldwide used in many movies, like *Home Alone*. Ukraine's musical influence extends into American popular music as well. George Gershwin's (1898-1937) classic song *Summertime* is believed by some music historians to have been inspired by the Ukrainian lullaby *The Dream Passes by the Windows*, performed by a Ukrainian National Chorus led by Oleksandr Koshetz (1875-1944) in New York.

While debated, this connection highlights the often-overlooked ways in which Ukrainian music has echoed across genres and continents. The country has also produced a remarkable lineage of world-renowned classical musicians. Sviatoslav Richter (1915–1997), one of the 20th-century's greatest pianists, was born in Zhytomyr. Vladimir Horowitz (1903–1989), another legendary pianist, hailed from Kyiv, and Emil Gilels (1916–1985), famous for his powerful yet lyrical playing, was born in Odesa/Odessa. Ukraine is also the birthplace of Oleh Krysa (b. 1942), a distinguished Ukrainian-American violinist born in Lviv, known for his expressive style and international performances.

Also, the internationally recognised composer Sergei Prokofiev (1891–1953) was born in the Donetsk region of Ukraine. Finally, there is one more outstanding musician worth noting: Serhii Bortkevych (1877–1952), also spelled Sergei Bortkiewicz in the Polish/German tradition due to his family's ancestry. The Ukrainian spelling, Bortkevych, reflects his national origin. He is often referred to as the last Romantic composer. His life, which crossed borders internationally, mirrored the turbulent history of the first half of the century. Despite the hardships he endured, Bortkevych's music remains powerful and optimistic.

Serhii Bortkevych was born on February 28th, 1877, into a wealthy family in Kharkiv, a major regional city located about 26 kilometres from what is now the Russian border. At the time, Kharkiv was an important cultural and educational centre of the Russian Empire, and in 1805 it became home to one of the empire's earliest universities: the Imperial University of Kharkiv.

Serhii was a second son. His parents had a family estate in Artyomovka village about 40 kilometres away from the city. Although Russian was the language spoken in Kharkiv at that time, the people in the villages of Kharkiv region spoke Ukrainian. Serhii often listened to their singing when he was young, spending time at the family estate in Artyomovka. He took piano lessons as a child, and when he was old enough to attend, he studied law at the University of St. Petersburg, the capital of the Russian Empire, on his father's suggestion.

At the time, jurisprudence was considered a stable and respectable profession—many young men pursued it for security, including the composer Pyotr Tchaikovsky (1840–1893), who studied law and even worked at the Ministry of Justice for several years. Like others of his generation, Serhii Bortkevych (1877–1952) also studied law; but his true passion was music. Whilst enrolled in law school, he simultaneously attended classes at the Imperial Conservatory, learning from renowned composers such as Anatoly Lyadov (1855–1914) and Karel Pieter Hendrik van Ark (1839–1902). It was not uncommon in that era to pursue two majors—one that promised financial stability, and another that nourished the soul, even if it brought little material reward.

During his student years, Bortkevych travelled with friends through Turkey, Greece, Italy, and Austria, combining their shared interest in the arts with sketching and drawing expeditions. Influenced by one of his university professors, he decided to continue his education in Germany. In February 1899, a wave of student unrest disrupted studies at St. Petersburg University, delaying his graduation by a year. During this time, he was also conscripted into the army but was discharged due to illness, returning to his family's home in Kharkiv to recover. After regaining his health, he enrolled in the Leipzig Conservatory in 1900, where he studied music under Alfred Reisenauer (1863–1907), a renowned German pianist and composer.

Upon graduating in 1902, Bortkevych was recognised as one of the top students in his class and was awarded the prestigious Schumann Prize. In the summer of 1904, he married Elizaveta Geraklitova, a close friend of his younger sister. Later that year, the couple moved to Berlin, where Bortkevych gave private piano lessons, performed in concerts, and continued to compose music.

The couple occasionally travelled to Italy and France, but would often return to his parents' home in Ukraine during the summer months. During his studies and early professional life in Germany, Bortkevych formed many lasting friendships. One notable example was his close bond with the distinguished Dutch pianist Hugo van Dalen (1888–1967), whom he met in

Berlin; their friendship endured until the end of Bortkevych's life. Among the works Bortkevych composed during his Berlin years was *Étude No. 8 in D-flat major* (Op. 15), a piece rumoured to charm its listeners—especially women. With two of his friends reportedly having met their future wives through performances of this piece, Bortkevych jokingly referred to himself as a musical "matchmaker."

Bortkevych's *Piano Concerto No. 1* in B-flat major (Op. 16), also composed during his time in Berlin, was met with great acclaim. It premiered in the Netherlands in the autumn of 1913, performed by his friend Hugo van Dalen, and was subsequently played by the Blüthner Orchestra in Berlin later that winter. The concerto reached American audiences when it was performed at Carnegie Hall in 1915, further cementing Bortkevych's growing international reputation.

When World War I broke out in 1914, Bortkevych—then a subject of the Russian Empire—could no longer remain in Germany and was forced to return to his homeland. Back in Kharkiv, he continued giving private lessons and performing concerts, while also composing works including his violin and cello concertos. However, the outbreak of the Russian Revolution soon brought widespread upheaval. As the owner of farmland and a family estate, Bortkevych faced the threat of losing everything. To protect his family, he decided to leave their village of Artemivka near Kharkiv.

In 1919, after General Anton Denikin's White Army briefly regained control of the area, Bortkevych returned home, only to find that his house had been plundered. With little left, he and his wife relocated to Crimea, determined to leave the country altogether. In Yalta, they rented a small room with a piano on Darsan Hill, where Bortkevych could continue to compose. It was likely there, on the night before their departure, that he wrote *Nocturne No. 1* (Op. 24)—a poignant piece, composed in a room overlooking the moonlit coast.

Though he was preparing to leave behind everything he had ever known—his home, his country, and a once-comfortable life—the music he created in that moment radiates peace, beauty, and quiet resilience. It reflects not sorrow, but a spirit uplifted through art in the face of profound loss.

In the spring of 1919, British, Italian, and American ships entered Crimea to assist in the evacuation of refugees fleeing the Russian Civil War. When Bortkevych left his home in the Kharkiv region, he carried what had once been a fortune—around 1.5 billion rubles in cash—which, due to extreme inflation, had become virtually worthless scraps of paper. The couple did not even have enough money to purchase tickets for passage. Fortunately, with the generosity of others, they were allowed to board a steamboat called the *Constantine*.

Grateful for the assistance he received, Bortkevych later dedicated a piano piece to Lieutenant Commander Thomas Greenhow Williams Settle (1895–1980), a U.S. Navy officer who was instrumental in helping evacuate refugees from Yalta. The overcrowded ship departed for Turkey. Bortkevych later recalled that the usually rough Black Sea was, on that day, as calm as a pond—a rare serenity that may have ensured the ship's safe arrival.

Four days later, the ship arrived in Constantinople (modern-day Istanbul). It took ten more days before Bortkevych and his wife were granted permission to disembark. Having lost all of his property and wealth in Ukraine, Bortkevych arrived in Turkey with only his delicate hands—unfit for manual labour—a small bag of clothes, pages of handwritten music, and his remarkable musical talent. These were the only possessions he carried into his new life.

At that time, thousands of refugees from the collapsing Russian Empire were flooding into the Turkish capital, many fleeing the threat of execution or imprisonment. Former nobles, wealthy businessmen, scholars, and artists—all stripped of their status—were desperately searching for any kind of work to survive and provide for their families.

According to Oleksa/Alexis Hryshchenko, Ukrainian painter who arrived in Istanbul in the autumn of 1919, the city was shrouded in grey rain, stripped of its colours yet alive with movement[11]. As the ship approached the harbour, the skyline emerged from the mist like a faded memory. For a Ukrainian refugee who had lost everything, Istanbul was both foreign and mesmerising: a chaotic sanctuary where exiles from across the Russian Empire searched for footing. The distant call to prayer echoed through damp alleyways, mingling with the creak of ships and the weary steps of the displaced. In this restless city, shaped by sorrow but humming with life, survival slowly began to take form.

After arriving in Constantinople, Bortkevych and his wife stayed at the home of her cousin. They spent their days walking through the unfamiliar streets of the city, searching for work and a way to secure food. By chance, Bortkevych encountered Lieutenant Commander Thomas W. G. Settle once again — the same American naval officer who had assisted him during the evacuation from Yalta. Settle, recognising the struggling composer, welcomed him warmly, offered him a meal, and even lent him some money to help him get through the difficult early days in exile.

One day, Bortkevych discovered one of his own music manuscripts in a local music shop and was surprised to learn that he was already known in Turkey. The store owner introduced him to the court pianist of the Sultan, which opened doors for him to give private lessons and concerts. He soon earned enough to rent a small house with a piano — a lifeline for a composer. Thanks to his charm, talent, and ability to connect with others, Bortkevych performed at prestigious venues such as the American Robert College, the American Sailors' Club, and even gave a performance in the presence of Admiral Albert Parker Niblack (1859-1929), then commander of the U.S. Navy in European waters. His students included the daughters of Turkish aristocrats and the children of European and British diplomats. Invitations to embassy events followed, where his performances helped him build a strong social and professional network in exile.

---

11 Hryshchenko, Alexis. *Between East and West: Memoirs, Notes, Essays*. New York: The Ukrainian Academy of Arts and Sciences in the U.S., 1954.

While in Constantinople, Bortkevych befriended Madame Natalie Shaponitsch, the wife of the ambassador of the Kingdom of Serbs, Croats, and Slovenes (later Yugoslavia). She helped the composer and his wife secure visas to leave Turkey, and, in July 1922, they travelled via Sofia to Belgrade before settling in Austria. In heartfelt gratitude, Bortkevych composed and dedicated a musical piece to Madame Shaponitsch.

From 1922 to 1929, Bortkevych lived in Vienna and in Baden, a holiday resort town near the Austrian capital. In 1925, he successfully obtained Austrian citizenship. In Vienna, he reconnected with musicians and publishers known from his earlier years in St. Petersburg, some of whom helped introduce him to the city's musical circles. Thanks to these connections, he was offered a position that allowed him to resume his professional life and rebuild his career in exile.

During his years in exile, Bortkevych received continued support from old friends. His close companion, the Dutch pianist Hugo van Dalen (1888-1967), was supporting his music both personally and professionally, especially during Bortkevych's years of exile in Europe. Van Dalen premiered Bortkevych's *Piano Concerto No. 1* in the Netherlands in 1913 and continued to help organise performances of his work. Another important figure from his earlier, more peaceful years was the Czech violinist Frank (František) Schmitt (1892–1960), who also settled in Austria. Schmitt had endured a dramatic past: during World War I, he was captured by the Russian army and sent to Siberia, but managed to escape with the help of locals who recognised his musical talent. He later became a professor of music at the Kharkiv Conservatory, where he met his future wife, Tatiana Kharin, the daughter of a noble family.

Following the Russian Revolution, the Schmitts fled eastward and spent years performing across Siberia, the Russian Far East, and Manchuria. Their son Yaroslav was born during a tour in Indonesia. After travelling through Southeast Asia, Schmitt returned to Europe in 1922 and settled in Germany in 1923. However, due to the rise of Nazi influence, his family relocated to

Serbia in 1925. A year later, in 1926, he accepted an invitation to perform in Brazil, where he lived until 1959.

A musical reunion occurred in December 1922, when they performed Bortkevych's piano concerto together with the Prague Philharmonic Orchestra. As was often the case, Bortkevych dedicated the piece to someone meaningful—in this case, to Frank Schmitt, in gratitude for their enduring friendship and collaboration.

In the spring of 1923, Serhii met Paul Wittgenstein (1887–1961), brother of the Austrian-British philosopher Ludwig Josef Johann Wittgenstein (1889–1951), whose work on language, logic, and meaning profoundly influenced 20th-century philosophy.

Paul Wittgenstein, a talented pianist and member of a prominent Viennese family and an older brother of Ludwig, was drafted into the Austro-Hungarian army during World War I. He lost his right arm in combat in the territory of modern Ukraine, an injury that seemed to end his career at the piano. Struggling with depression and a loss of purpose, he eventually resumed music with the support of his family. At their request, Serhii composed the *Piano Concerto No. 2 in B-flat major, Op. 28*, written specifically for the left hand alone. Wittgenstein purchased the exclusive rights to the piece and premiered it in Vienna in November 1923. However, the concerto was not published during Bortkevych's lifetime, and Wittgenstein did not allow anyone else to perform it. Bortkevych's work joined a small but notable repertoire of left-hand piano compositions written for Wittgenstein, including pieces by Maurice Ravel (1875–1937) and Sergei Prokofiev (1891–1953), all commissioned by the Wittgenstein family.

In 1930, Serhii Bortkevych composed another work for Paul Wittgenstein—the *Russian Rhapsody, Op. 45*, originally written for left-handed piano and orchestra and later adapted for two hands. Wittgenstein, unusually for a Western musician of the time, gave performances in the Soviet Union during the early 1930s. While touring the region, he remarks about his tour at Soviet Ukraine and the butter shortages he faced while staying in hotels for foreigners. These observations, made during the devastating Holodomor famine of 1932–1933, offer a rare Western account of the humanitarian crisis that unfolded under Soviet rule.

Beginning in 1928, Bortkevych divided his time between Paris and Berlin, remaining active in both cities' musical circles. However, when the Nazi regime rose to power in Germany in 1933, individuals labelled as "Russians" — a term broadly applied to many émigrés regardless of their actual ethnicity — were increasingly excluded from public cultural life. Facing discrimination and professional isolation, Bortkevych had no choice but to leave Berlin and return to Vienna at the end of that year. From then on, he spent his winters in Vienna and summers in the nearby spa town of Baden.

During the 1930s, the Bortkevych family faced serious financial hardship. To survive, Serhii relied on performing, teaching private lessons, and publishing his compositions. Seeking an additional source of income beyond his musical manuscripts, he undertook the task of translating the correspondence between Pyotr Tchaikovsky and his patron, the businesswoman Nadezhda von Meck, into German. His close friend Hugo van Dalen later edited the text for Dutch readers. The book was published in 1938 and attracted wide public attention, offering a unique glimpse into the personal and artistic world of one of Russia's most revered composers.

Bortkevych's *Ten Preludes* gained popularity in Vienna, often performed at Sunday concerts by Paul de Conne (1874–1959), a distinguished Russian concert pianist and teacher of German origin, best known as a pupil of Anton Rubinstein (1829–1894). Thanks to these performances, Bortkevych's name gradually spread through Viennese musical circles. On February 7th, 1937, in celebration of his 60th birthday, the Vienna Symphony Orchestra performed one of his works live on a Viennese radio channel, with Bortkevych himself conducting. The event marked a rare moment of public recognition during a period of otherwise modest acclaim and financial uncertainty.

In February 1938, Hugo van Dalen organised a concert in the Netherlands showcasing Bortkevych's work, which received considerable attention and seemed to mark a turning point in his international recognition as both pianist and composer. Just as Bortkevych began to hope for a more stable and quiet life, those hopes were abruptly shattered when, on March 13th, 1938, Germany annexed Austria in the event known as the Anschluss. The political shift would once again cast uncertainty over his future and threaten the fragile security he had rebuilt in Vienna.

Later, Bortkevych spent several months in Yugoslavia, but returned to Vienna in December 1939, where he remained throughout World War II. Life during the war years was extremely difficult. His German publishing house in Leipzig, which had printed most of his music manuscripts, was destroyed in a heavy air raid in December 1943. As a result, Bortkevych lost a vital source of income. Some of those lost materials were only rediscovered decades later, during the 2010s. Despite the hardship, he managed to survive with food and financial assistance from his devoted friend Hugo van Dalen in the Netherlands and a Dutch female pianist. Even in these trying circumstances, Bortkevych continued to compose. His *Piano Sonata No. 2, Op. 60*, performed in Vienna in November 1942, reflects his deep love for his Ukrainian homeland, as well as his personal struggles and spiritual reflections.

At the end of the war, as Soviet forces bombed Vienna and entered the city in the spring of 1945, Bortkevych narrowly escaped death on several occasions. During one particularly harrowing moment, when Soviet soldiers attempted to throw grenades into the cellar of his apartment building, Bortkevych reportedly shouted in Russian from within. Recognising the language, the soldiers refrained from attacking. His quick thinking is said to have saved not only his own life, but also the lives of his neighbours who were sheltering with him in the cellar.

After the war, Bortkevych was officially reinstated as an Austrian citizen. He had first acquired Austrian citizenship in 1925, following his relocation to Vienna and with the support of close friends. However, during the Anschluss in 1938, all Austrian citizens were considered part of the German Reich, and Borkevych's legal status became uncertain. It was only after the end of World

War II that his Austrian citizenship was formally restored. In the autumn of 1945, his financial situation improved when he was appointed head of the educational department at the Vienna Conservatory. He continued to compose and conduct with various orchestras until his death on October 25th, 1952. Having lived through the Russian Revolution and both World Wars, Bortkevych spent much of his life in exile, moving across countries to survive. He never returned to his native Kharkiv or the village of Artyomivka. He is buried in the Vienna Central Cemetery, where his grave remains a quiet tribute to his remarkable and resilient life.

Serhii Bortkevych's relationship to Ukrainian identity appears shaped more by cultural proximity than by overt national allegiance. Born into a wealthy family in Kharkiv—a city that, at the time, was a major hub of the Russian Empire—he was raised in a Russified elite environment. However, his family's estate in the nearby village of Artyomovka brought him into regular contact with Ukrainian-speaking communities and their folk traditions. As a child, he listened to village songs and was exposed to the rhythms and melodies of rural Ukrainian life, experiences that would later leave an imprint on his compositions. Although he studied law and music in St. Petersburg and moved in circles aligned with Russian imperial culture, his musical style retained traces of Ukrainian folk influence, particularly in its lyricism, modal colour, and pastoral sensibility. In this sense, Bortkevych exemplifies the complex layering of identity characteristic of many figures in the late imperial borderlands—rooted geographically in Ukraine, culturally hybrid, and artistically shaped by both imperial and local traditions. His work reflects how Ukrainian musical culture could subtly persist, even in artists who did not explicitly frame themselves in national terms.

Today, Bortkevych's music is increasingly gaining recognition around the world. His scores are preserved in archives in Germany, the Netherlands, and other countries, and many of his works are now freely accessible on platforms like YouTube. In Ukraine, however, his name remained relatively unknown until the early 21st-century. In 2001, Mykola Sukach, chief conductor of the Ukrainian Academic Symphony Orchestra "Philarmonia", was introduced to Bortkevych's music by renowned Ukrainian pianist Mykola Suk. That same year, Sukach conducted *Symphony No. 1: From My Homeland* for the first time in Ukraine. The work reveals the deep and complex musical influences that shaped Bortkevych as a composer in exile — drawing richly from Ukrainian folk songs and Cossack dance rhythms, it serves as a poignant tribute to the land he never stopped loving.

Mykola Sukach developed a deep admiration for Bortkevych's music. He began collecting the composer's published manuscripts whenever he encountered them abroad and became a tireless advocate for reviving Bortkevych's legacy in Ukraine through performances and recordings. In 2008, Ukrainian pianist Pavlo/Pavel Gintov, based in the United States, released a CD of Bortkevych's works[12] and has since performed them widely across the U.S. Reflecting on Bortkevych's style, Gintov noted: "Bortkevych was a brilliant pianist, so he composed music that pianists can play easily and skillfully. It is very pleasant to play his compositions. He created melody lines well. Long melodies sound natural in the expanse, and sometimes there are unexpected twists and turns. The dramatic works are so lyrical." [13]

Despite living through some of the darkest chapters of the 20th-century, Bortkevych composed music that radiates warmth, hope, and lyrical beauty. Rooted in Ukrainian folk melodies, his style was shaped by the Romantic traditions of Franz Liszt (1811–1886) and Frédéric Chopin (1810–1849), as well as the grandeur of the Russian classics — particularly Pyotr Tchaikovsky (1840–1893), who spent his summers in Ukraine, and Nikolai Rimsky-Korsakov (1844–1908), whose family was of Ukrainian descent. His years of study in Germany also exposed him to the powerful influence of Richard Wagner (1813–1883), which left a mark on his orchestration and harmonic language. These varied influences formed

---

12 *Bortkiewicz: Piano Works*. Performed by Pavel Gintov. Piano Classics (Brilliant Classics), 2017, compact disc.
13 Interview with Pavlo Gintov, 13th February 2021.

the foundation of a musical voice that, despite exile and personal loss, remained remarkably joyful and expansive.

What makes Bortkevych's legacy even more touching is his practice of dedicating works to those who supported him — friends, patrons, fellow musicians — ensuring their names would live on through his music. Listening to his compositions today, one hears not only the beauty of his melodies, but also an enduring message: that even in times of turmoil, we must hold onto hope. His music is a testament to resilience — and a quiet encouragement from the past to the present.

The Poetry of Colour
The Vibrant World of Sonia Delaunay
(14.11.1885-05.12.1979)

The vivid colour in Sonia Delaunay's artwork is unforgettable. I never tire of looking at her paintings — they offer new inspiration each time. There is something familiar in the feminine touch of spring and summer tones that radiate from her canvases. Though widely celebrated as a French painter and designer, Sonia was born in Ukraine.

In 1964, she became the first living female artist to have a solo exhibition at the Louvre Museum. I have encountered her works in various settings — from the Thyssen-Bornemisza National Museum in Madrid to the Russian Avant-Garde exhibition at the National Gallery of Australia in Canberra — and have been deeply impressed by the way her talent transcends national borders. She was one of the pivotal figures of both the first and second waves of abstract art, and tracing her life offers insight not only into modernism but into the story of a woman who translated colour into language.

Looking at Sonia Delaunay's vibrantly coloured paintings or the dazzling dresses she designed, one might never guess how complex and dramatic her early life was. She was born in 1885 into a Ukrainian Jewish family and given the name Sarah Shtern. Her exact place of birth remains uncertain. Some sources cite the cosmopolitan port city of Odesa/Odessa, while others point to the much smaller town of Hradyzk in what is now the Poltava region. According to synagogue records in Odesa/Odessa, her maternal grandfather lived in the city, and his daughter Hana gave birth to a girl named Sarah on November 1st, 1885. Still, all official biographies list her birth date as November 11th. Her father, Elias, an energetic man five years older than Hana, worked as a foreman in a nail-making factory. Sonia deeply admired him.

While both locations are now within Ukraine, the question of Sonia Delaunay's birthplace remains significant in how we understand and describe her as Ukrainian. Odesa/Odessa, at the time, was a largely Russian and Yiddish-speaking cosmopolitan city, and many Jews born there are more often culturally identified as Russian rather than Ukrainian. Hradyzk, by contrast, was a much smaller and more provincial town, surrounded by ethnically Ukrainian villages, and located in the Poltava region, where nearly half the population spoke Ukrainian according to the 1897 census. We do not know exactly how Delaunay understood or negotiated her identity in relation to Ukrainian, Russian, and Jewish cultural frameworks, but it is likely that she embodied a hybrid identity shaped by her Ukrainian-Jewish background. While it is reasonable to assume she was exposed to Ukrainian folk culture—such as traditional weddings and songs—her cultural world was more firmly rooted in Yiddish and Russian, especially given that she was raised in her uncle's affluent, Russian-speaking household in St. Petersburg. Delaunay's linguistic choices, her cosmopolitan ambitions, and her eventual name change all suggest a conscious effort to leave behind the provincial identity of the Ukrainian-Jewish shtetl and align herself with a broader, international modernity centred in the cultural capitals of St. Petersburg, Paris, and beyond. The ambiguity surrounding her birthplace—whether due to lost records or deliberate omission—further underscores the complexity of her self-creating and raises broader questions about how we define "Ukrainian" identity in such fluid, imperial contexts.

Sonia's early family life was marked by emotional distance and disruption. While she was deeply attached to her father, her mother was preoccupied with her younger son and maintained a complicated, often cold relationship with Sonia. After her father's death and the family's resulting financial hardship, five year old Sonia was taken in by her maternal uncle, Henri Terk—a wealthy, childless lawyer in St. Petersburg. Her mother reportedly objected to his wish to adopt the girl, but Henri's household would become a formative refuge. In gratitude, Sonia would later adopt the surname "Terk" as her pen name.

Henri Terk was not only a successful legal figure but also a respected intellectual in the imperial capital. He sat on the editorial board of a major Russian encyclopedia and was surrounded by a circle of cultured friends and artists. Under his roof, Sonia was introduced to a world of ideas, refinement, and artistic appreciation. Her summers were often spent travelling across Europe, where she was profoundly moved by the works of Henri Matisse (1869-1954), Carolus-Duran (1837-1917), Paul Gauguin (1848-1903), and others she encountered in museums. At her girls' school in St. Petersburg, she showed strong abilities in mathematics—so much so that some teachers encouraged her to pursue the sciences. However, it was her art teacher who recognised her true talent and urged her to study art abroad.

At the age of 18, Sonia enrolled at the State Academy of Fine Arts in Karlsruhe, Germany, a university town near the French border where some of her uncle's relatives lived. Founded in 1854, the Academy was well regarded in Germany and later counted among its alumni notable artists such as Georg Baselitz. Karlsruhe had long-standing ties to Russian and Slavic culture—writers like Fyodor Dostoevsky (1821-1881) and Vasily Zhukovsky (1783-1852) had visited the city, and Dostoevsky even referenced it repeatedly in his works. The Russian author Ivan Turgenev (1818-1883), who lived in Germany in the 1860s, also had his work published there by a Russian-language press. Immersed in this intellectually rich environment, Sonia was exposed to European modernist ideas that would deeply influence her evolving artistic vision.

While studying in Germany, Sonia became increasingly drawn to the vibrant artistic life of Paris, which was then the epicentre of modern art. In 1905, she moved to the French capital, where she encountered the works of Van Gogh, Gauguin, and the bold experimentation of the Fauves—young artists known for their vivid colours and expressive techniques. Not eager to return to St. Petersburg after finishing her studies, she sought a way to secure personal and artistic freedom. One option, unconventional but strategic, was marriage.

Though not considered conventionally beautiful by the standards of the time, Sonia had a strong sense of personal style and a disarming warmth that made her memorable. Around this time, she became close to Wilhelm Uhde (1874-1947), a German art critic and collector known for promoting Picasso (1881-1973) and the Naïve School. Recognising her talent, Uhde encouraged Sonia to exhibit her work and supported her entry into the Parisian art world. In 1908, at age 23, Sonia married Uhde in London. The marriage may have been one of mutual convenience—beneficial for Sonia's legal and social standing in France, and for Uhde, who, as was later widely believed, sought to maintain appearances due to his homosexuality. Though the marriage was short-lived, it provided Sonia with the stability and autonomy she needed to begin building her name in Parisian artistic circles.

Within a year, Sonia left her husband and began a relationship with the talented young French painter Robert Delaunay (1885-1941). They met through Robert's mother, Rose, who styled herself Comtesse de Rose and was a regular visitor to Sonia's exhibitions—often accompanied by her son. Like Sonia, Robert came from a fractured family; his parents were divorced, and he had been raised by his grandfather. Perhaps it was this shared experience of a lonely childhood, along with their mutual passion for art, that sparked their deep connection.

As Sonia searched for her own artistic style, she was influenced by the prevailing movement of Cubism[14], but she also brought her natural affinity for mathematics into her exploration of colour and form. She learned a great deal from Robert, who was

---

14   Cubism is an early 20th-century art movement (1907-1917) pioneered by Pablo Picasso and Georges Braque, characterised by fragmented forms, multiple perspectives, and geometric abstraction, marking a departure from traditional linear perspective.

described as "a poet who wrote not with words but with colours." Together, they developed a new artistic language—painting with vivid, contrasting colours that energised and defined each other. Rather than blending, the colours in their work were meant to coexist dynamically. For both Sonia and Robert, colour was not merely a tool—it was life itself.

In 1911, Sonia and Robert welcomed their only child, a son named Charles. For her newborn, Sonia sewed a patchwork quilt of red and yellow squares—an object that today is seen as a turning point in her artistic development. The quilt resembled the colourful, handmade coverings used by families in the Ukrainian countryside, where Sonia had spent the early years of her life. Whether she recalled these folk motifs from childhood or reconnected with them later as a subconscious memory, the act of recreating them in a Parisian context suggests more than just maternal care—it marked the beginning of a new visual language. The quilt, now on display at the Musée National d'Art Moderne in the Centre Pompidou, blends folk tradition with modernist abstraction, much as Nikolai Gogol (Mykola Hohol) (1809-1852) had once drawn on Ukrainian folk life to captivate urban readers of the Russian Empire. In Sonia's case, one might even say that she participated in the globalisation of Ukrainian cultural forms— translating the memory of domestic, rural aesthetics into a radically modern art movement in the heart of cosmopolitan Paris.

While mutually influencing each other, Sonia and her husband Robert Delaunay developed a distinctive style evolving from cubism, which the French poet Guillaume Apollinaire (1880-1918) famously named "Orphism." This movement emphasised the expressive and dynamic use of colour, in contrast to the more spiritual and philosophical abstraction associated with painters like Wassily Kandinsky (1866-1944). The Delaunay's became central figures in the European avant-garde, admired for their bold visual language.

Sonia quickly recognised that colour was her greatest strength as an artist. She would later reflect that her innate sense of colour came from childhood memories of Ukrainian landscapes, the vivid embroidery of folk costumes, and the joyful visual culture of traditional weddings. These formative impressions — however distant from her Parisian present — remained a wellspring of inspiration throughout her life. In this way, she, like writers such as Hohol/Gogol, brought elements of Ukrainian folk culture into cosmopolitan artistic conversations, giving them new form on a global stage.

Sonia also demonstrated remarkable emotional intelligence and social savvy. She maintained a respectful friendship with her ex-husband Wilhelm Uhde, who had supported her early career and collected works by both Sonia and Robert. She had a remarkable gift for forming and sustaining lasting connections — an asset in the fast-paced, competitive world of early 20th-century Parisian art. Her ability to forge and nurture enduring relationships was one of the many reasons she thrived in the artistic circles of early 20th-century Europe.

In addition to painting, Sonia ventured into book illustration while in Paris. Encouraged by the poet and art critic Guillaume Apollinaire (1880–1918), she began to explore new ways of blending text and image. Around this time, she met the Swiss-French writer Blaise Cendrars (1887–1961), whose dynamic and avant-garde poetry resonated with Sonia's vibrant visual language. Their collaboration resulted in the groundbreaking 1913 work *La Prose du Transsibérien*, a two-metre-long accordion-folded book combining Cendrars' poetry with Sonia's vividly coloured abstract designs. The work caused a stir for its experimental format and was seen as a unique fusion of visual art and literature — a bold step forward in modernist art.

Sonia also had a vivid memory of witnessing the 1905 Russian Revolution while visiting her uncle's family in St. Petersburg. That early exposure to political and social upheaval stayed with her, shaping her understanding of art as something alive, responsive, and intertwined with the world around her.

Although Sonia was surrounded by avant-garde artists — many of whom struggled financially — she was fortunate to remain financially secure, thanks to the continuing support of her uncle Henri Terk, a prominent lawyer in St. Petersburg. This allowed her to maintain a comfortable lifestyle and to focus on her art without commercial pressure, travelling freely across Europe in search of inspiration.

When World War I broke out in 1914, Sonia and her family left Paris and relocated to Madrid. They also spent the warmer months in neighbouring Portugal, as her husband Robert found the Spanish summers unbearable. For Sonia, the Iberian Peninsula became a revelation. She was deeply moved by the vivid colours, music, and emotional intensity of everyday life in Spain and especially Portugal. These new impressions resonated with her memories of the bright textiles and festive traditions of her Ukrainian childhood. This exposure marked the beginning of a new artistic chapter—one in which she developed a colour language that was even more vibrant, expressive, and rhythmically dynamic, reflecting the fusion of cultural impressions from both Eastern Europe and the Iberian world.

When the Russian Revolution broke out in 1917, Sonia Delaunay lost the financial support she had long received from her uncle Henri in St. Petersburg. Faced with the need to become financially independent, she turned her artistic vision toward applied arts. Drawing on her distinctive aesthetic, she began designing accessories such as umbrellas, handbags, and scarves featuring bold, geometric patterns. From there, she expanded into fashion.

In Madrid, where she was living during the war years, Sonia quickly gained a reputation as an innovator. She opened her own fashion house, *Casa Sonia* (Sonia's House), which became a popular destination for the Spanish elite. Her innovative and colourful designs resonated with the avant-garde and the fashionable upper class alike. A famous photograph from the time even shows all three princesses of the Spanish royal family dressed in Sonia's creations—an emblem of her rising fame and the appeal of her wearable art.

Eventually, Sonia Delaunay broadened her creative pursuits beyond painting, transforming her vibrant aesthetic into a versatile design language. She applied her bold, rhythmic patterns to a wide range of objects—from accessories and quilts to playing cards, tableware, and even automobiles. One of her most iconic collaborations was with Citroën, for which she designed a model of the B12 car. A now-famous photograph shows a woman driver standing beside the Delaunay-designed car, wearing a matching outfit—an early and striking example of what we would now call a "total design" approach. Though only in her 30s, Sonia had already established herself as a savvy businesswoman with an uncanny ability to blend art, fashion, and commercial enterprise.

During her years in Spain, Sonia also became acquainted with Russian émigré intellectuals and artists who had fled the country after the 1917 revolution. Among them were Russian composer Igor Stravinsky (1882-1971), known for his bold rhythms and shifting harmonies and a ballet dancer Vaslav Nijinsky (1889-1950), a choreographer born in Kyiv, was celebrated for his extraordinary technique and emotive performances and an impresario and a visionary Russian art critic Sergei Diaghilev (1872-1929). Sonia met Diaghilev—then based in Monaco—while he was performing in Spain in 1918. Their meeting led to her collaboration with his famous *Ballets Russes* (1909—1929), for which she created sets and costumes for the production of *Cleopatra*. Her interdisciplinary talents gained further recognition, and by 1920, her work was featured in solo exhibitions in cities such as Stockholm, Bilbao, and Berlin.

In 1921, Sonia and Robert Delaunay returned to Paris, where they reconnected with the city's vibrant cultural scene, particularly the poets and artists of the Dada movement. Sonia began collaborating with a Romanian and French avant-garde poet Tristan Tzara (1896-1963), famously designing a dress embroidered with his poetry—an innovative fusion of visual art and literature that helped catapult her into the world of high fashion. Over time, she developed more than 50 distinct textile patterns, which were produced in a factory in Lyon. By 1924, she had opened her own fashion atelier, *Maison Sonia*, in Paris. Her clientele included wealthy aristocrats, industrialists, and intellectuals drawn to her unique designs. Sonia's dresses—crafted from silk, wool, tulle, and other materials—were wearable works of modernist art, bold in both pattern and form. Unlike many designers of her day, she often wore her own creations, embodying the artistic spirit she brought to life through fabric.

At the 1925 Paris Exposition Internationale des Arts Décoratifs et Industriels Modernes, Sonia Delaunay's vibrant works—from paintings and textiles to costumes and fashion—drew widespread acclaim, cementing her status as a central figure in the emerging Art Deco movement. Her boldly coloured, rhythmic designs gained international attention, and her influence extended beyond visual art into academia, as she was invited to lecture at the prestigious Sorbonne University. Her 1920s dress sketches, full of dynamic colour contrasts and elegant modernity, captured the spirit of the time with both flair and innovation.

She also expanded her creative reach into interior design, where her work was marked by a distinct harmony of geometric patterns and vibrant colour combinations. In 1928, she published a book titled *Fabrics and Carpets*[15], showcasing her textile work—many of which echoed the folk motifs and rich textures found in traditional Ukrainian countryside carpets. Two years later, in 1930, she released another influential volume, *Structure, Colour, Idea*[16], articulating the theoretical foundation of her artistic vision.

Sonia Delaunay's unique style—a harmonious fusion of modernist structure and avant-garde flair—left a profound mark on interwar fashion. With the outbreak of World War II, she relocated to the south of France, where she faced a personal loss: her husband, Robert Delaunay died of cancer in a French Montpellier in October 1941. To honour his legacy, she later sold their home in order to finance a solo exhibition of his work, though friends generously allowed her to remain there until the war's end. Ever attuned to the cultural zeitgeist, Sonia had a rare ability to anticipate and shape evolving trends. By 1950, she was collaborating with major abstract artists such as Jean Arp (1886–1966) and Al-

---

15 Sonia Delaunay, *Tapis et tissus* (Paris: Éditions d'Art Charles Moreau, c. 1929). This publication featured a portfolio of textile designs and was pivotal in highlighting the relationship between fine and applied arts in her work.
16 Sonia Delaunay, *Compositions, couleurs, idées* (Paris: Éditions d'Art Charles Moreau, c. 1930). This book outlined her artistic philosophy, especially her emphasis on simultaneity in colour theory and abstraction.

berto Magnelli (1888-1971) on a series of lithographs, further extending her influence into the postwar modernist movement.

In recognition of her contributions to the arts, the French government awarded Sonia Delaunay the Legion of Honour in 1974. She outlived both her husband and her son—surviving Robert by 30 years—and continued working in her atelier almost until her death in 1979 at the age of 94. Her son, Charles (1911-1988), became a noted jazz critic, though their relationship was often strained; he died a few years before she did. Reflecting on her extraordinary life, one might say that Sonia lived several distinct lives: one in the Russian Empire before the revolution; another as a student and emerging artist in Germany and France; a chapter as an artistic entrepreneur in Spain and Portugal; a shared creative partnership with her husband Robert; the role of a devoted, if sometimes challenged, mother; and, throughout it all, a full and independent life as a woman and an artist.

Sonia expressed the world through colour and spent her life believing that colour was life itself. She is said to have once remarked, "Colour is the skin of the world," remaining true to her boundless curiosity and inner child throughout her career. She combined the power of colour, energy, and rhythm to create a new artistic universe she called "colour rhythm." From paintings and book illustrations to fabrics, ties, scarves, bags, dresses, swimsuits, ceramics, car designs, home interiors, and exhibition spaces—everything she touched became a canvas for this vision.

Sonia was also a brilliant marketer. She launched her own business, and even registered *Simultané* as her trademark, turning her sense of beauty into a recognisable and influential brand. Her creativity knew no boundaries, and her artistic self found expression across media, genres, and everyday life. In doing so, Sonia Delaunay not only created art—she lived it.

This ambiguity about Delaunay's origins—urban versus provincial, Odesa/Odessa versus Hradyzk—is more than a historical footnote. It reflects a deeper tension in how we interpret identity in a multiethnic empire like the Russian one, and how we define what it means to be "Ukrainian" within such a context. Born in the Russian Empire's Pale of Settlement, Sarah/Sonia likely grew up speaking Russian and possibly Yiddish—not Ukrainian—and there is little evidence that she actively identified with Ukrainian national or cultural life before leaving for St. Petersburg, and later, Paris. Like many ambitious Jews of her generation, her path was upward and outward—from shtetl or port city to imperial centre, from local roots to a universal stage. Changing her name and immersing herself in French and German culture was part of a broader project of reinvention.

It is unclear whether she downplayed her birthplace from a desire to shed provincial associations, personal reinvention, or simply the result of incomplete documentation. What we do know is that the landscapes of both Poltava and Odesa/Odessa shaped her early life—one provincial and largely Ukrainian-speaking, the other cosmopolitan and dominated by Russian and Yiddish. While she may not have been part of explicitly Ukrainian cultural circles, her hybrid background—Jewish, imperial, multilingual—adds a valuable and complex thread to the tapestry of Ukraine's contributions to global modernism.

Delaunay's life and work challenge us to think beyond rigid national categories. Her journey—from a borderland Jewish girl named Sarah to a Parisian modernist named Sonia—underscores the fluidity of identity in the early 20th-century. Like others in this volume, her story urges us to reconsider what "Ukrainian-ness" really means: is it defined by ethnicity, birthplace, language, or memory? Perhaps the more honest answer is not to choose, but to allow these layers to coexist.

Sonia Delaunay embraced her many selves—shifting nationality, language, even her name—never confining herself to one style, one genre, or one identity. She lived fully and freely, savouring the richness of the world. And when you look at the vivid colours of her paintings, you might see a glimmer of the Ukrainian summers of her childhood. If you ever find yourself in Paris, stroll past 16 Rue Simon—and remember Sonia, her boundless creativity, and the radiant energy she gave to the world.

A Statesman of Conscience
Mykhailo Tereshchenko
(30.03.1886-01.04.1956)

Mykhailo Tereshchenko was born in Kyiv into a prominent Ukrainian family with Cossack roots and a strong tradition of entrepreneurship and public service. One of his ancestors helped introduce sugar production technology to Ukraine, building a factory and amassing significant wealth. His great-grandfather Artemiy Tereshchenko displayed business acumen from an early age, beginning his career as an errand boy in a shop in Hlukhiv — once the capital of the Cossack Hetmanate. He eventually rose to become the store's manager and earned such a reputation for financial savvy that locals nicknamed him "Karbovanets", a term that referred to the currency of the time. Artemiy's early success laid the foundation for a family legacy of enterprise and philanthropy that would shape Mykhailo's life and values.

At the time, Napoleon Bonaparte had prohibited the import of sugar from Britain and encouraged the development of sugar beet processing within France. While stationed in France as a part of Cossack unit, Artemiy Tereshchenko learned the techniques of beet sugar production. Upon returning to his native Ukraine, he applied this knowledge to establish one of the region's earliest sugar factories. In parallel, he also ran a successful salt business — purchasing salt on the Crimean Peninsula and distributing it throughout central and eastern Ukraine.

During the Crimean War (1853–1856), Artemiy and his son Mykola further expanded their wealth by supplying food to the Russian Imperial Army and providing lumber for naval shipbuilding. Artemiy's sugar enterprise grew into one of the largest and most successful in the Russian Empire.

In March 1870, Emperor Alexander II granted Artemiy the title of nobility in recognition of his contributions to agricultural development. However, according to imperial tradition, men over 70 were exempt from personally bowing before the Tsar to receive the honour. Seizing this opportunity—and likely motivated by Cossack pride—Mykola Tereshchenko formally received the title of hereditary nobility on behalf of his elderly father. Behind this gesture was a quiet yet symbolic act of resistance: the Tereshchenkos, descendants of Ukrainian Cossacks, held a deep sense of national dignity and were unwilling to bow to the Russian emperor.

This episode also reflects a broader historical shift in the relationship between the Ukrainian Cossack elite and the Russian imperial establishment. In the 18th-century, Catherine the Great had actively blocked the ennoblement of both the Polish szlachta and many Ukrainian Cossack families, whom she considered too low in social standing. However, by the 19th-century, families like the Tereshchenkos—with their growing wealth and influence—were able to navigate this barrier and attain noble status. Their story illustrates not only economic upward mobility but also the gradual fusion of Ukrainian Cossack identity with the Russian imperial nobility, a process that blended loyalty to the empire with a quiet preservation of national pride.

In contrast to the often-rigid gender norms of the era, women were treated with notable respect and affection in the extended Tereshchenko family. In 1882, Symon Tereshchenko, one of Artemiy's three sons, commissioned a renowned French horticulturist to cultivate a new variety of rose in honour of the woman he wished to marry. The result was a unique flower named Madame Olympe Terestchenko, adopting the French spelling of the family name. Although few descendants of the family remain today, this elegant rose variety continues to appear in French flower catalogues, serving as a living tribute to both a personal love story and the family's cultural legacy.

The Tereshchenko family coat of arms is rich in symbolism that reflects both their Ukrainian identity and civic ideals. Featuring a blue and yellow shield — the colours that would later become the national flag of Ukraine — it was officially approved in the late 19th-century by the Russian emperor. Two lions holding stalks of wheat flank the shield, symbolizing industrial strength and agricultural prosperity. At its base appears the family motto: *"Стремлением к общественным пользам"* (Aspiring for the common good), a phrase that captures the Tereshchenko legacy of philanthropy, enterprise, and public service.

Although written in Russian, the motto reflects a broader European tradition. Similar ideals appeared in Latin phrases such as "pro bono publico" (for the public good) and "salus populi suprema lex esto" (let the welfare of the people be the supreme law), showing how the Enlightenment value of civic duty was shared across cultures and adapted into Imperial Russian noble identity. Long before blue and yellow became a national banner, these colours had already been embraced by the Tereshchenkos as a symbol of their vision for their family and Ukraine's future.

The yellow and blue colours on the Tereshchenko family coat of arms were no coincidence. They represented a conscious expression of their Ukrainian identity and reflected their values — the golden wheat fields and blue skies of their homeland, hard work, generosity, and a dedication to the common good. Securing the emperor's approval for a coat of arms bearing these colours in the late 19th-century signified that the choice was both intentional and of symbolic significance.

The Tereshchenko family estate in Kyiv was located near the railway station, and from a young age, Mykhailo Tereshchenko (also spelled *Mikhail* in Russian) was fascinated by the trains coming and going. He loved to dream about travel — and thanks to his family's wealth and lifestyle, he was able to do it early in life. At the age of 11, he moved to a villa his family had built in Cannes, in southern France, where they relocated for the sake of his father's health and the milder climate. When he turned 16, Mykhailo returned to Kyiv to take the entrance examination for Kyiv Gymnasium for Boys No. 1.

The following year, however, Mykhailo's life changed dramatically. His grandfather Mykola Tereshchenko (1819–1903) passed away in Kyiv, and just a month later, his father, Ivan Tereshchenko (1854–1903), died of tuberculosis at their villa in Cannes. Suddenly, at a very young age, Mykhailo inherited not only great wealth, but also significant responsibility — including 70,000 rubles, a sugar refinery, and a valuable art collection.

Ivan, who lacked business acumen, had been excluded from the family's commercial ventures by his father, Mykola. Instead, he devoted himself to art and philanthropy, building an impressive collection. He also served in the military at a young age and became close to Vasily Vereshchagin (1842–1904), the renowned painter known for his depictions of war and service in the Russian Imperial Navy. Tragically, Vereshchagin died at the battleship *Petropavlovsk* in April of 1904 during the Battle of Port Arthur, one of the early and decisive events in the Russo-Japanese War (1904–1905).

After the death of his grandfather and father, two uncles took care of Mykhailo Tereshchenko until he came of age at 20. After graduating from Kyiv Gymnasium for Boys No. 1, he went on to study economics and law at the University of Leipzig in Germany. There, he was deeply influenced by his professor of statistics and the subject itself, which convinced him that the Russian Empire urgently needed to modernise its economy.

In 1905, the wave of social unrest that would later be called the First Russian Revolution swept the empire. Even the Tereshchenko family sugar refinery was affected, as workers joined the uprising. These events sparked Mykhailo's growing interest in politics and reform.

In the autumn of 1906, he travelled to England to study commercial law and finance. His cheerful personality and open-mindedness won him many friends, including the son of the Rothschild family, who would later become a prominent banker. He became fascinated with the British system of constitutional monarchy, and began to believe that a modern constitutional model — with checks on imperial power — would be better suited for Russia than the existing autocracy. It was during this period that he first began to seriously consider a political career.

Ever since his university days in Germany, Mykhailo Tereshchenko spent his summer vacations at his late father's villa in the south of France, frequently visiting Paris and Monaco to attend ballets, theatre performances, and operas — and occasionally trying his luck at the casino.

In the early summer of 1907, in Paris at the age of 21, he met and fell in love with a French woman named Margaret Noé. His mother, who was then living in St. Petersburg, strongly opposed the idea of her son marrying a foreigner who did not belong to the Orthodox faith. Despite her disapproval, Mykhailo continued seeing Margaret in secret.

Later, Mykhailo Tereshchenko studied law at Moscow University, and in 1911 he passed the bar exam, officially qualifying to practice as a lawyer. The family owned a house in St. Petersburg, and Mykhailo fully embraced the cultural and social life of the imperial capital. He became friends with the poet Alexander Blok (1880–1921), and together with his sisters, he founded a publishing house called *Sirin*. Although the publishing venture was not financially successful, it was a conscious investment in the cultural life of the era.

In its first three years, the *Sirin* publishing house released works by poets who defined the literary trends of the time — Andrei Bely (1880–1934), Alexander Blok (1880–1921), and Valery Bryusov (1873–1924) — later known as representatives of the Russian Silver Age of poetry. In this way, Mykhailo fulfilled the philanthropic principle set by his grandfather Mykola Tereshchenko, who had urged that 80% of family profits should support art and culture.

He became a regular guest at the Mariinsky Theatre and developed close friendships with legendary figures such as opera singer Feodor Chaliapin (1873–1938) and ballerina Anna Pavlova (1881–1931). As a highly educated and cosmopolitan young man with inherited wealth and cultural influence, many sought his company. A portrait of Mykhailo was painted by the Russian artist Aleksandr Golovin (1863–1930), who at the time worked in stage design at the Mariinsky. That portrait is now part of the Baltic Exhibition collection at the Malmö Art Museum in Sweden.

When Mykhailo Tereshchenko's uncle Oleksandr passed away in October 1911, Mykhailo personally transported his body from St. Petersburg to Kyiv for burial, honouring the family tradition of laying their loved ones to rest in their native land. His arrival came just weeks after the assassination of Russian Prime Minister Pyotr Stolypin (1862–1911) on September 14th, 1911, at the Kyiv Opera Theatre during a performance of *The Tale of Tsar Saltan* by Rimsky-Korsakov, in the presence of Tsar Nicholas II. Stolypin died four days later from his wounds. This event left the city under heightened security. Despite the tense atmosphere, Mykhailo was determined to fulfill his duty. Motivated by a desire to revive the rich cultural life he had known in Paris and St. Petersburg, and to elevate Kyiv's artistic scene, he began supporting major cultural initiatives. He donated to the founding of the Kyiv Conservatory and the Operetta Theatre and contributed to the restoration of the Kyiv Opera House—laying the foundation for the city's future as a centre of musical and theatrical excellence.

Mykhailo Tereshchenko had a taste for luxury, and in 1912 he discreetly purchased the 127-metre *Iolanta*, then the world's longest cruise ship, originally built for the Italian royal family. To avoid public attention, the transaction was made under his mother's name. The yacht was intended for a deeply personal purpose: to transport his frail younger brother from the family's villa near city of Feodosia in Crimea to their residence in Cannes for the holidays, as his brother's health made train travel impossible. The ship's Norwegian captain would later play a crucial role in Mykhailo's life, ultimately helping him escape danger following the Russian Revolution.

Mykhailo Tereshchenko, born into a prominent Ukrainian family, was deeply committed to supporting Ukrainian culture through generous philanthropy—funding institutions such as the *Kyiv Conservatory* and championing education and the arts. Culturally, he identified strongly with Ukraine, but politically, he operated within the structures of the Russian Empire and later the Provisional Government, where he served as Foreign Minister during the pivotal year of 1917. In this role, he faced growing demands from national movements, particularly from the Ukrainian Central Rada, which declared autonomy in June 1917. Tereshchenko initially resisted full Ukrainian autonomy, fearing it would fracture the unity of the state amid wartime instability. He favoured a federative model for the empire but prioritised central control to maintain order. Ultimately, his government recognised the Central Rada in a limited way through a compromise (The First Universal), though only under significant pressure. Tereshchenko represented a form of imperial liberalism: he believed in modernisation and cultural pluralism within a unified, reformed Russia, but he did not support full independence or radical political decentralisation for Ukraine.

Although Mykhailo's mother continued to strongly oppose his marriage to Margaret, the couple moved together to St. Petersburg in the summer of 1913. In early 1917, after Margaret gave birth to their daughter, Mykhailo presented her with an extraordinary gift—a diamond necklace. He had purchased a 150-carat rough blue diamond in Antwerp, which was later cut and crafted into a necklace by Cartier. The result was a striking pear-shaped, blue-toned gem weighing 42.92 carats, which became known as the *Tereshchenko Blue*. At the time, it was the second-largest blue diamond in the world.

World War I, which began on July 28th, 1914, gradually eroded Mykhailo Tereshchenko's confidence in the Russian Imperial government, particularly due to its lack of military decisiveness. As wartime expenses mounted, he shut down his publishing house, scaled back cultural patronage, and redirected his focus toward politics. He became a regular attendee at Freemason meetings, where he connected with like-minded reformers, including lawyer Alexander Kerensky (1881–1970)—his future colleague in the Provisional Government—and engineer Nikolay Nekrasov (1879–1940). The three men, close in age and shaped by international education, shared liberal ideals; like Tereshchenko, Nekrasov had studied in Germany, though he specialised in bridge-building technologies.

At the end of 1916, Grigori Rasputin (1869-1916), a mystic who held significant influence over the Russian imperial family, was assassinated by nobles who feared his growing political power. Soon after, in February 1917, mass strikes erupted in Petrograd (formerly St. Petersburg), marking the beginning of the February Revolution. On March the 12th, when Tsar Nicholas II (1868-1918) ordered the dissolution of the State Duma, sections of the military, including the Volynsky Regiment, mutinied rather than suppress the demonstrators. Amid this chaos, Duma deputies including Alexander Kerensky (1881-1970), Nikolay Nekrasov (1879-1940), and Vasily Shulgin (1878-1976) met with Duma Chairman Mikhail Rodzianko (1859-1924) to assume leadership.

Mykhailo Tereshchenko, then just 30 years old, played a critical role by intervening directly with the rebellious Volynsky Regiment—many of whom, like Tereshchenko, were of Ukrainian origin. Notably, Rodzianko, Shulgin, and Tereshchenko had all been born in Ukrainian lands, reflecting Ukraine's active role in the revolutionary events. Tereshchenko sent a telegram declaring that the Duma had taken power, overriding the Tsar's dissolution order.

On March the 15th, the Provisional Government was formally established, and Tereshchenko was appointed Minister of Finance. Realising the army had turned against him, Nicholas II abdicated, backdating the act to mask the pressure he faced and protect the future of his son, Tsesarevich Alexei (1904-1918). He named his brother, Grand Duke Michael Alexandrovich (1878-1918), as successor—but Michael declined the throne, ending the three-century-long Romanov dynasty.

Russia's participation in the First World War had devastated its economy, and by 1917 the newly established Provisional Government faced severe financial strain. As Minister of Finance, Mykhailo Tereshchenko sought emergency funding to stabilise the economy and continue supporting the war effort. He successfully raised millions of rubles in government bonds, including contributions from his former classmate from the Rothschild family and from Jacob Schiff (1847-1920), a prominent American banker and philanthropist, as well as other international sources[17]. In today's value, these contributions would amount to several hundred million U.S. dollars. However, after the Bolsheviks seized power in October 1917, Lenin's government refused to recognise or repay these debts, leaving international investors uncompensated. Tereshchenko, who fled into exile, carried the personal and diplomatic consequences of this financial rupture for years afterward.

In the spring of 1917, Mykhailo Tereshchenko replaced Pavel Milyukov (1859-1943) as Minister of Foreign Affairs in Russia's Provisional Government. His primary task was to maintain diplomatic relations and alliances with Great Britain and France during a period of intense instability. As Foreign Minister, Tereshchenko suspected Vladimir Lenin of being a German agent and launched a covert investigation into his activities. However, the effort was compromised when the Justice Minister of the Provisional Government leaked the information to the press during the summer, effectively stalling the inquiry. By early October 1917, sentiment within the Provisional Government had shifted, with many advocating for peace negotiations with Germany. Tereshchenko, however, firmly opposed such moves — likely influenced by a lingering mistrust of Germany dating back to his student years there. As Petrograd grew increasingly volatile, intellectuals and government officials began leaving the city. Tereshchenko, however, remained behind with his wife, who was pregnant, and their ten month old daughter. On the morning of November the 6th (October 24th, Old Style), the Bolsheviks launched their coup, swiftly occupying government buildings, post offices, and train stations, marking the onset of the October Revolution.

On that fateful day, a final peace proposal was once again delivered via the Austrian Embassy, prompting the Provisional

---

17 See Naomi W. Cohen, *Jacob H. Schiff: A Study in American Jewish Leadership* (Hanover, NH: Brandeis University Press, 1999), 199-203.

Government to convene a cabinet meeting at the Winter Palace. However, by then, decisive action was no longer possible. Alexander Kerensky had already left Petrograd the night before, leaving Mykhailo Tereshchenko to preside over what would become the last meeting of the Provisional Government. That evening, the signal gun fired from the cruiser *Aurora* marked the start of the Bolshevik assault on the Winter Palace. The palace was soon stormed, and Tereshchenko, along with other ministers, was arrested and taken to the Peter and Paul Fortress on the Neva River — ironically just across the water from his family's estate in the heart of the former imperial capital.

According to legend, his wife Margaret survived the chaos of the Bolshevik takeover only because she had fainted from shock upon hearing of her husband's arrest. Mistaken for dead by the invading soldiers, she was left unharmed.

When Pavlo Skoropads'kyi (1873–1945) became Hetman of Ukraine (April–December 1918), his pro-landowner policies likely enabled the temporary restoration or preservation of some Tereshchenko family assets, particularly in the Poltava, Chernihiv, and Kyiv regions. Although detailed records are scarce, his regime aimed to reverse earlier socialist land redistributions and stabilise private property. Both Skoropads'kyi and Mykhailo Tereshchenko came from elite Ukrainian families with Cossack heritage and shared a European education and cultural ties to Ukrainian identity. However, they followed divergent political paths: Tereshchenko, a liberal reformer, served as Foreign Minister in Russia's Provisional Government and supported a federated Russian state with limited autonomy for Ukraine; Skoropads'kyi, under German patronage, proclaimed Ukrainian sovereignty during his rule. While no evidence suggests direct collaboration between the two, their shared background and status within Kyiv's, as well as St. Petersburgh's elite circles, make it likely they were at least familiar with one another. Any restoration of the Tereshchenko estates under the Hetmanate was short-lived, swept away by the upheavals that followed.

The Russian Revolution brought a dramatic end to Mykhailo Tereshchenko's life as a politician and millionaire, plunging him into years of hardship. He lost his entire fortune during the upheaval. His mother and wife made desperate efforts to secure his release from prison, using every possible connection and remaining funds, but their attempts met great resistance. Tereshchenko was charged with espionage, and Vladimir Lenin reportedly held a personal grudge against him — stemming from Tereshchenko's earlier role in launching an investigation into Lenin's ties to Germany. As it became clear, Mykhailo had made numerous political enemies during his time in government, and they now closed in on him during the shifting tides of power.

This story, drawn from family accounts, adds a dramatic and symbolic dimension to Mykhailo Tereshchenko's escape from Bolshevik imprisonment. While some details — such as a direct negotiation between Margaret Tereshchenko-Noé, Lenin, and Trotsky, or the exchange of the *Tereshchenko Blue* — are not verified in archival sources and may lean toward legend, they reflect the chaos and desperation of the revolutionary period.

According to the Tereshchenko family's account, Margaret Tereshchenko-Noé managed to enter the prison under the guise of assisting a French journalist who was seeking an interview. She then secured a meeting with Vladimir Lenin to plead for her husband's release. During the conversation, she offered the *Tereshchenko Blue* diamond — originally a gift from her husband — as a ransom. Lenin refused to accept it, but later that night, Lev Trotsky (1879–1940) reportedly contacted her and proposed an exchange: the diamond in return for Mykhailo Tereshchenko's life, citing the Bolsheviks' urgent need for funds to build their army. The diamond was delivered through the French embassy, and Tereshchenko was subsequently allowed to board a train bound for Murmansk. From there, he crossed into Finnish territory and by March 1918 had reached safety in Norway. While archival evidence on this episode remains limited, it has been preserved within the Tereshchenko family as a defining story of courage, sacrifice, and survival during one of history's most turbulent moments.

Having barely escaped with his life, Mykhailo Tereshchenko experienced a profound shift in worldview. Though he had lost his fortune, status, and political influence, he found deep gratitude in the simple fact of freedom. The wealth and luxury he once knew in the Russian Empire no longer held the same value. Eager to distance himself from both his opulent past and the collapse of his political career, he sought peace and anonymity. For a time, he settled in Trondheim, Norway — the hometown of the Norwegian captain who had once commanded his private cruise ship — and there he began the slow process of recovery from the upheaval of revolution and exile.

In April 1918, Margaret joined Mykhailo Tereshchenko in Norway, and the couple officially married at the end of July. Hoping to build international support against the Bolsheviks, Tereshchenko applied for visas to the United States, the United Kingdom, and France, but was denied entry to all three. Margaret moved to Paris, while Mykhailo remained in Norway. He had hoped to meet U.S. President Woodrow Wilson but failed to gain access. On July 11th, 1918, *The New York Times* published an interview titled "Tereshchenko Warns Against Support for Red Russia,"[18] in which he urged Western governments not to legitimise Bolshevik rule and warned of the dangers of their expansionist ideology. Believing that Admiral Alexander Kolchak (1874-1920) might lead a successful counter-revolution, Tereshchenko travelled to Murmansk to meet him, but Kolchak never arrived. Disillusioned by the collapse of the old political order, he returned to Norway. After the end of World War I in November 1918, Tereshchenko — now a stateless former minister — faced ongoing threats to his safety living a life of uncertainty, moving frequently between Oslo and Stockholm in the early years of his exile.

His mother, Elizaveta, died in 1923, a few years after she had successfully escaped Bolshevik Russia and settled in France, where she lived out her final years in exile. Around the same time, Mykhailo's personal life also reached a turning point — after sever-

---

18 "Tereshchenko Warns Against Support for Red Russia," *The New York Times*, July 11, 1918.

al years of separation and the strains of revolution, displacement, and exile, his marriage to Margaret ended in divorce in 1923.

Tereshchenko had little choice but to liquidate his villa in southern France and sell his beloved cruise ship to begin repaying the debts he had incurred borrowing from the Rothschilds to support the Provisional Government. Wherever he went, the financial burden haunted him. Fortunately, his time in Norway and Sweden introduced him to influential contacts — including the Swedish banker Marcus Wallenberg Sr. (1864–1943), who played a key role in founding Electrolux and a precursor to Scandinavian Airlines. Wallenberg secured Tereshchenko a position at the bank affiliated with the shipping firm A.F. Klaveness & Co. Though a far cry from serving as Russia's Minister of Finance, Tereshchenko accepted the role without hesitation. His resilience and financial expertise eventually led to a position with Creditanstalt (officially *Österreichische Creditanstalt für Handel und Gewerbe*) in Vienna. Founded in 1855, by Anselm von Rothschild as the Viennese branch of the Rothschild family, this financial institution was established to promote trade and industrial development across the Habsburg Empire. At Creditanstalt, Mykhailo Tereshchenko played a significant role in guiding the bank through a period of notable growth and stability during the interwar years, drawing on his financial expertise and international connections to support its expanding operations.

Mykhailo Tereshchenko was also a gifted linguist, fluent in English, German, French, Italian, Czech, Norwegian, and Portuguese, in addition to Ukrainian, Russian, Latin, and Ancient Greek. After the Russian Revolution, many former elites from the Russian Empire clung to their imperial identities and refused to adopt new nationalities, often living as stateless persons. Unlike many émigrés, however, Tereshchenko did not succumb to despair after losing nearly 15,000 works of art, his immense fortune, and his political career. Instead, he remained optimistic and actively engaged in the post-imperial financial world. With his deep knowledge of banking and wide international network, he played a key role in managing the affairs of remaining Russian financial institutions abroad and earned broad respect across European financial circles.

The evolving spelling and usage of Mykhailo Tereshchenko's name throughout his life offers a compelling lens through which to examine his complex identity and adaptation in his life. In imperial Russian circles, he primarily went by Mikhail (Михаил), the standard Russian form of his name. This was expected for a member of the nobility and political elite in the Russian Empire, where Russian was the dominant administrative and cultural language. In exile, however, the spelling of his name varied depending on the context and country: in Western Europe, especially in France and Norway, he was often referred to as Michel or Mikhail Tereshchenko, depending on the language of the publication or official record. Some documents and publications also use the French-influenced transliteration "Michel Terestchenko." Ukrainian sources today generally restore his name as Mykhailo, aligning with Ukrainian linguistic norms and national historiography. There's no definitive evidence that he legally changed the spelling himself, but the evolution in usage reflects the fluidity of his identity — a Ukrainian aristocrat, a Russian imperial official, and later a stateless exile navigating French, Scandinavian, and international environments. The fact that he never rigidly stuck to one version underscores his multinational, adaptable character, shaped by empire, revolution, and exile. This multilingual, multi-spelling reality also speaks to a deeper ambiguity: he was a Ukrainian patriot culturally, a Russian politician administratively, and a European liberal intellectually — a man caught between overlapping and shifting worlds.

In 1926, while living in exile, Mykhailo Tereshchenko met Ebba Holst, a young Norwegian woman ten years his junior. Ebba came from a well-connected family — her father owned Oslo's Grand Hotel, and her mother was originally from Chicago. Despite Mykhailo's charm, intelligence, and cultured background, Ebba's parents were deeply sceptical of the match. To them, Tereshchenko was an older man burdened by the weight of a collapsed empire, political exile, and financial hardship. Hoping to end the relationship, they sent Ebba to Chicago for a year of study, convinced that time and distance would erase her attachment.

But it did not. The bond between Ebba and Mykhailo endured, and in 1929, the two were officially married in Paris. At the time, Tereshchenko already had a daughter and a son from his previous marriage to Margaret Noé. The new union brought him a sense of renewal—something he had not known since the revolution uprooted his entire world. In the autumn of 1931, Ebba gave birth to a son named Ivan. For Mykhailo Tereshchenko, this moment was profoundly meaningful. Naming his son Ivan—a traditional name that echoed both his father's name and their family heritage—reflected a deep connection to his roots, even as he built a new life far from Ukraine. Ivan's birth symbolised a fresh start after years of exile, upheaval, and personal loss. Surrounded by his second wife and young son, Mykhailo felt he had regained a piece of the stability and happiness that had once defined his pre-revolutionary world.

After Mykhailo Tereshchenko's exile, particularly in the 1920s and 1930s, he had few to no significant ties with organised Ukrainian political émigré movements. This is notable, especially considering his cultural background and elite Cossack heritage. Despite his deep cultural ties to Ukraine and a long record of philanthropy that supported Ukrainian institutions before 1917, Mykhailo Tereshchenko did not align himself with the Ukrainian nationalist movements that gained momentum in exile after the Russian Revolution. Politically, he belonged to the liberal-reformist camp of the Russian Provisional Government and envisioned a federated Russian state rather than a fully independent Ukraine. This stance diverged sharply from the goals of émigré Ukrainian leaders tied to the Central Rada, the Hetmanate, or the UNR governments-in-exile, who prioritised national sovereignty. After fleeing Russia, Tereshchenko gravitated toward Western European financial and diplomatic circles—particularly among French, Norwegian, Swedish, and Jewish banking elites—and shifted his focus toward professional stability and rebuilding a personal life disrupted by revolution and exile. He worked in institutions like Creditanstalt, leveraging his linguistic skills and international experience. His quiet professionalism and moderate liberal worldview distinguished him from political activists and made him a pragmatic exile rather than a nationalist one. His story highlights a broader theme: that Ukrainian identity in the early 20th-century was not monolithic, and individuals like Tereshchenko occupied a complex middle space between imperial liberalism and cultural nationalism.

In the early 1930s, Mykhailo Tereshchenko relocated to Vienna, where he took up a position managing a bank and reentered elite cultural circles. Among his acquaintances was Ferdinand Bloch-Bauer (1864–1945) an Austrian-Jewish industrialist, sugar magnate, and art patron of Secessionist movement, best known as the husband of Adele Bloch-Bauer and for his connection to Gustav Klimt's famous portraits of her, later referred to as the *Woman in Gold*.

Through Bloch-Bauer's salon, Tereshchenko encountered a range of artists, writers, composers, and intellectuals, as Vienna remained a hub of creative activity despite the darkening political horizon. The period was marked by mounting instability: Stalin's regime tightened its grip on the USSR, the man-made famine of 1932–1933 ravaged Ukraine, and the Nazi Party was surging in neighbouring Germany. Against this backdrop of the looming crisis, Tereshchenko remained focused on his professional responsibilities. Through steady work in the banking sector, he succeeded in repaying 99% of the substantial debts he had incurred during his tenure in the Russian Provisional Government—an extraordinary feat that reflected both his integrity and resilience.

On the eve of the Anschluss—Nazi Germany's 1938 annexation of Austria—Mykhailo Tereshchenko took strategic steps to preserve the assets of the Vienna-based bank where he worked. He relocated its financial operations to Monaco, where he helped establish, a new institution known as the Continental Management Company and became its first chairman. This venture is considered a prototype of the modern offshore bank, offering financial services beyond traditional regulatory jurisdictions.

Despite living in Monaco, Tereshchenko was still officially classified as a refugee of the former Russian Empire, which complicated his legal status and led to the denial of entry into the United Kingdom. When Monaco was invaded first by Italy and then by Germany during World War II, he relocated with was invaded first by Italy and then by Germany his family to a suburb of Lisbon, Portugal. There, he assisted with refugee relief efforts and was even offered a post in Mozambique, then a Portuguese colony in southern Africa.

In 1945, as the war came to an end, he was finally granted a British visa and moved to London. Though based in the UK, Tereshchenko remained active in African business ventures. Drawing on his financial and entrepreneurial experience, he advised on the coffee trade, acquired agricultural land in Mozambique, ran a palm oil company, and made annual business trips to Africa even into his 60s.

Mykhailo Tereshchenko passed away on April 1st, 1956, just one day after turning 70. Traces of the Tereshchenko family legacy — whose motto was "Aspiring for the common good" — can still be found in the heart of Kyiv. One of the most notable is the mansion at 12 Shevchenko Boulevard, now home to the great Ukrainian poet Taras Shevchenko's National Museum. Originally built by Mykhailo's grandfather, Mykola Tereshchenko, the grand residence was constructed in the Renaissance style and featured 47 rooms, each heated by one of 40 fireplaces, reflecting both the family's wealth and their deep cultural investment in Ukrainian civic life. The lives of Taras Shevchenko (1814–1861) and the Tereshchenko family symbolically intersect through a shared mission of serving the Ukrainian people. Although Shevchenko died before the Tereshchenkos rose to prominence as philanthropists and industrialists, his ideals — advocacy for dignity, national identity, and cultural awakening — inspired the kind of social responsibility that the Tereshchenkos embodied. That the house of Mykola Tereshchenko in Kyiv now houses the National Museum of Taras Shevchenko is profoundly symbolic: it represents the meeting point between the poet's prophetic vision and the concrete deeds of those who believed in culture as a force for public good. In this convergence lies the living continuity of Ukraine's humanistic and enlightenment tradition.

The house where Mykhailo Tereshchenko was born, located at Shevchenko Boulevard 34 in Kyiv, still stands today. This 26-room building in Venetian Gothic style once served as the office of the State Migration Service but has sadly fallen into disrepair and now teeters on the edge of collapse. Another landmark tied to the Tereshchenko legacy is the residence of Mykhailo's uncle, Fedir Tereshchenko, at 9 Tereshchenkivska Street. Originally built in a neoclassical style, it became the Russian Art Museum and is now the Kyiv Art Gallery. This building also holds significant historical importance: it served as the Ministry of Foreign Affairs for the Ukrainian State under Hetman Pavlo Skoropads'kyi between April and December, 1918. This was the period when the Central Rada had been dissolved and Skoropads'kyi, backed by German and Austro-Hungarian forces, assumed control and established a more centralised, conservative government in Kyiv. Later from August to December 1919 it became an office of General Anton Denikin's White Army, when the building served as the headquarters of his administration. These sites not only reflect the architectural and cultural contributions of the Tereshchenko family but also stand as silent witnesses to Ukraine's turbulent path through revolution, independence, and war.

Next door, at 15 Tereshchenkivska Street, lived Mykhailo's aunt Varvara, who—together with her husband—had been, like his father, a renowned art collector. After the Revolution, Varvara made every effort to protect the Tereshchenko family's vast art collection. However, in 1921, it was expropriated by the Soviet authorities. All that remained to her was the attic of her former home and a job as a janitor in her own home. Even in that diminished role, her movements and activities were strictly controlled. She passed away the following year, in 1922.

The house at 15 Tereshchenkivska Street, now home to the Bohdan and Varvara Khanenko National Museum of Arts, exemplifies the values of the Tereshchenko family. Though modest in its late 19th-century exterior, the interior reveals an opulence inspired by Italian palaces—a reflection of the idea that life was meant to be quietly enjoyed rather than ostentatiously displayed. The home's discreet elegance suggests a belief in inward happiness and cultured living, while the family's philanthropic legacy demonstrates a deep commitment to improving public life. In Kyiv alone, the Tereshchenkos sponsored the construction and development of the St. Volodymyr Cathedral, the Operetta Theatre, the National Art Gallery of Ukraine (formerly the Kyiv City Museum), and the Kyiv Polytechnic Institute. Mykhailo's grandfather, Mykola Tereshchenko, also established the Tereshchenko Foundation, which supported six hospitals, including a 280-bed facility for the poor and homeless in Kyiv.

Seeing former Tereshchenko properties transformed into public museums, libraries, and cultural institutions is a powerful reminder that their family motto—"Aspiring for the common good"—was more than just words. It continues to shape lives today, just as Mykhailo Tereshchenko did in his own time.

Mykhailo Tereshchenko's Ukrainian identity was cultural and familial rather than political. Born in Kyiv into a wealthy Ukrainian family with Cossack roots, he inherited a legacy of entrepreneurship and philanthropy deeply tied to Ukraine. The Tereshchenkos supported major Ukrainian institutions and consciously expressed their national identity—most notably through their Cossacks imaged blue-and-yellow coat of arms and commitment to the public good.

Though Tereshchenko identified with Ukrainian culture, he was politically aligned with liberal imperial reform. As Foreign Minister in Russia's Provisional Government, he supported a federated empire and opposed full Ukrainian independence. In exile, he distanced himself from nationalist politics but remained connected to his heritage. His life reflects the complexity of Ukrainian identity in the early 20th-century—rooted in culture, shaped by empire, and marked by global engagement.

Incidentally, Mykhailo Tereshchenko's legacy continue unfolding through his grandson, Michel Tereshchenko, a descendant of Mykhailo and his first wife, Margaret Noé. After Ukraine gained independence in 1991, Michel returned to the family's ancestral homeland and founded a business in Hlukhiv, the historic

Cossack town closely associated with the Tereshchenko family. Embracing his Ukrainian heritage and the family's enduring motto—"Aspiring for the common good"—Michel became an active participant in civic life and was elected and served as a mayor of Hlukhiv between 2015 and 2020. He also authored a book reflecting on his grandfather's life and legacy, helping to revive public memory of a remarkable figure whose influence spanned empires, revolutions, and continents.

The life of Mykhailo Tereshchenko stands as a vivid reflection of the upheavals and contradictions of the 20th-century. Born into immense wealth and privilege in a Ukrainian family rooted in Cossack traditions, he rose to prominence as a liberal reformer, philanthropist, and statesman in the final years of the Russian Empire. His life crossed paths with revolution, exile, loss, and reinvention—yet through all of it, he remained guided by ideals of public service, cultural enrichment, and international engagement. Though his political vision ultimately did not align with the rise of Ukrainian independence movements, his contributions to Ukrainian cultural life and his sense of responsibility to society leave a legacy that transcends politics. The buildings, institutions, and memories tied to the Tereshchenko name—especially in Kyiv and Hlukhiv—serve as living reminders of a family that chose to invest its fortune not only in grandeur, but in the enduring value of the common good.

From Imagination to Flight
The Life of Igor Sikorsky
(25.05.1889-26.10.1972)

The helicopter with the callsign *Marine One*, used to transport the President of the United States, was invented by Igor Sikorsky[19], a Kyiv-born aviation pioneer. Born in 1889 into an esteemed family, Igor was the son of Ivan Sikorsky (1842-1919), a professor of medicine at Kyiv University and a renowned psychiatrist. His godfather was Grand Duke Pyotr Nikolaevich Romanov (1831-1891), a cousin of Russian Emperor Alexander III, and his baptism took place in the grand St. Volodymyr Cathedral, one of Kyiv's most iconic churches built with the sponsorship of the Tereschchenko family. Ivan Sikorsky, who had earlier worked in a hospital in St. Petersburg, maintained friendships with many influential cultural figures, including the celebrated artist Viktor Vasnetsov (1848-1926). Vasnetsov later contributed to the interior decoration of the Volodymyrsky Cathedral and is said to have painted the face of St. John (Ioan) to resemble Ivan Sikorsky himself. Coming from a long line of Orthodox clergy, with both Ivan's father and grandfather being priests, the Sikorsky household blended deep religious roots with a loyalty to the Russian monarchy. Ivan's upbringing in a religious school and his monarchist beliefs shaped the values of the family in which Igor grew up.

Although Igor Sikorsky is often described as a "Russian-American" inventor, due to his own statements and the cultural affiliations of his family, he was born and raised in Kyiv—then part of the Russian Empire, now the capital of Ukraine. His family belonged to the imperial intelligentsia and aligned culturally with Russian Orthodox and monarchist values, rather than with the rising Ukrainian national movement of the early 20th-century. Sikorsky himself rarely referred to a distinct Ukrainian identity

---

19 In Ukrainian, his name would be rendered as Ihor Sikorskyi, but here I use the spelling Igor Sikorsky as he himself wrote and published it in the United States.

and would likely have considered himself Russian in a cultural sense. Still, in a 1933 letter to a friend, written after his immigration to the United States, he emphasised that "My family, which originated in a village in the Kyiv region where my grandfather and great-grandfather were priests, has purely Ukrainian roots."[20]

Igor Sikorsky's grandfather, Oleksii, was an Orthodox priest in the village of Liubcha in Kyiv/Kiev gubernia. His son, Ivan, who later became a prominent psychiatrist, married the well-educated Zinaida Temriuk-Cherkasova. They raised five children, including Igor. It was very common back then for those from a clerical background, mainly children of priests to pursue education and scholarly careers. Notably, Ukrainian historians such as Ukraine's first president Mykhailo Hrushevsky (1866 – 1934) and famed Cossack historian Dmytro Chyzhevsky (1894 – 1977) also came from priestly families.

However, Igor's formative years unfolded on Ukrainian lands, and his legacy is deeply tied to the educational and scientific institutions of Kyiv. In acknowledging Sikorsky as part of Ukraine's historical landscape, this chapter also recognises that his life and achievements were shaped in part by the multicultural, multiethnic setting of Ukraine – then and now.

The Sikorsky family lived near the Golden Gate in Kyiv, at what is now Yaroslaviv Val Street 15B. Igor was the youngest of five siblings – three older sisters and an older brother – and was

---

20 From a letter by Igor Sikorsky to Vasyl Halych, USA, 1933. In: Igor Sikorsky: From Kyiv to Connecticut, from Sky to Heaven, ed. by I. Shpak, Kyiv: ADEF-Ukraine Publishing House, 2014, p. p.12. (in Ukrainian)

deeply cherished by his family. Raised in a privileged environment, he was given room to nurture his curiosity and creativity. His mother, Maria, a music lover and avid reader, introduced him to Leonardo da Vinci's sketches of flying machines, sparking a lifelong fascination with flight. In 1896, when Kyiv University hosted a conference on natural sciences and medicine, seven year old Igor watched in awe as kites and balloons soared above the nearby grounds. It may have been then that his childhood dream of flight first took shape. Fascinated by physics, he built a home workshop where he crafted prototypes and mechanical toys. By age 12, he had constructed a working motor. He devoured the science fiction of Jules Verne and often dreamed of walking inside an enormous airship, its interior finished in walnut wood—a dream that, decades later, would take tangible form in the machines he created.

In 1900, Igor Sikorsky enrolled in the *Boy's Gymnasium No. 1* in Kyiv, now home to the Faculty of Philology at Kyiv University. Notably, writers Konstantin Paustovsky (1892-1968) and Mikhail Bulgakov (1891-1940) were also educated there, though at different times. The school's strong emphasis on the humanities left Igor, who was drawn to science and mechanics, largely unengaged. In 1903, he transferred to the naval academy in St. Petersburg, following his older brother's path, but again found it unfulfilling. Determined to become an engineer, he sought a more technically focused education. After a brief stint in a French school—cut short by the turmoil following the 1905 Russian Revolution—he returned to Kyiv. In 1907, he entered the Mechanical Faculty of the newly established Kyiv Polytechnic Institute, an ambitious institution modelled after France's École Polytechnique and supported by Russian Finance Minister Sergei Witte (1849-1915). The school emphasised both theory and practice, offering programs in science, agriculture, and engineering design to prepare students to improve societal living conditions. There, Igor joined the aeronautical club and began conducting early aviation experiments that would lay the groundwork for his later innovations.

During the winter holidays of 1909, Igor Sikorsky (1889–1972) travelled to Paris to purchase an aircraft engine, funded by his father and his sister Olga. While there, he spent time with French aviation enthusiasts and met Ferdinand Ferber (1862–1909), one of the early pioneers of aviation in Europe. Ferber, a French military officer and a strong proponent of flight, helped popularise the work of Otto Lilienthal and the Wright brothers in France, and his ideas deeply influenced young Sikorsky.

In Paris, Sikorsky acquired a 25-horsepower, three-cylinder engine modelled after the design of Alessandro Anzani (1877–1956), an Italian engineer and motorcycle racer whose lightweight engines had powered several important early flights—most famously, Louis Blériot's 1909 crossing of the English Channel. Returning to Kyiv with the engine, Sikorsky continued working with the aeronautical club at the Kyiv Polytechnic Institute, building several prototypes over the following years and honing his engineering skills through hands-on experimentation.

At the same time, another Ukrainian aviation pioneer, Fedir Tereshchenko (1888–1950), also a graduate of Kyiv Polytechnic Institute and cousin of Mykhailo Tereshchenko (1886–1956), became one of the first aeroplane designers and manufacturers in the Russian Empire. He founded an aircraft workshop in his estate in the Zhytomyr region, where he developed and produced a series of aircraft under the "FT" (Fedor Tereshchenko) brand, including reconnaissance and training planes. His early contributions to the aviation industry, like those of Sikorsky, show how Ukraine played a notable role in the formative era of global aviation.

Igor Sikorsky envisioned placing two 180-kilogram engines on either side of a plane to increase lift and stability. However, he lacked engines powerful enough to carry a man. Determined to solve this problem, he returned to France to purchase two more advanced engines. This endeavour was supported by his friend Fedor Bylinkin, the son of a merchant who financed the trip, and Vasyl Yordan, a fellow student from the Kyiv Polytechnic Institute. Together, they constructed a biplane called *BIS-1*, named using the initials of their surnames—Bylinkin, Igor (Sikorsky), and Yordan. Although *BIS-1* failed to take flight, their second prototype, *BIS-2*, successfully flew approximately 600 metres on June the 10th, 1910, marking Sikorsky's first real step into aviation history. That same year, Igor witnessed a pivotal moment when Sergei Utochkin (1876–1916), a pioneer of Russian aviation who had flown a French biplane in 1909, visited Kyiv. During a flight demonstration at the local hippodrome — the site where the Dovzhenko Film Studio now stands — Sikorsky was inspired by Utochkin's performance. This experience further strengthened his resolve to design an aircraft that could not only fly but also set new standards in engineering and performance.

Although Igor's family poured a fortune into his dream of building aeroplanes, his academic performance suffered as a result. At the Kyiv Polytechnic Institute, even a single "C" (considered a failing grade) could prevent a student from graduating. While his classmates were preparing their final theses, Igor was spending his days in the workshop. With the full support of his family, he made the bold decision to drop out of university and devote himself entirely to aviation.

Between 1911 and 1912, he constructed *Aircraft No. 4* and *No. 5*. The latter was showcased during a flight demonstration in Kyiv, where its success caught the attention of Emperor Nicholas II, who was present at the event. Igor even had the opportunity to speak directly with the Russian tsar.

Despite not having a university diploma, Igor's contributions to aviation did not go unnoticed. In April 1912, after his *Sikorsky 6A* performed successfully at an aircraft exhibition in Moscow, he was awarded a medal by the Imperial Russian Technical Society for his pioneering research and for inventing his own aircraft model.

The Russo-Baltic Wagon Factory in St. Petersburg recognised Igor Sikorsky's talent and purchased the patent for his *Sikorsky 6A* aircraft. At just 22 years old, he was offered the prestigious position of chief engineer at their aviation division. In April 1912, Igor relocated to St. Petersburg to begin this new chapter. During his years in Kyiv, in addition to working on aeroplanes, he also experimented with other flying machines. Notably, in 1910 he constructed a "flying sled" and refined it through several iterations, eventually developing a third model.

Igor Sikorsky deeply valued the people who worked alongside him, and when he moved to St. Petersburg, he brought his invention team from Kyiv with him. There, he continued to innovate, working on the *Sikorsky 6B, 7,* and *8* models. In just two years, he designed and built 20 new aircraft. Among these was a groundbreaking large-scale model — *Sikorsky No. 9* — which laid the foundation for his future aviation designs. Up to that point, most aeroplanes used only a single engine, but Sikorsky's *No. 9* was the first in the world to feature multiple engines. He named the aircraft *Russki Vityaz* (Russian Knight). This revolutionary design paved the way for the creation of large bombers and eventually passenger planes. In recognition of his achievement, Emperor Nicholas II personally awarded Sikorsky a gold pocket watch. The *Russki Vityaz* marked the beginning of Sikorsky's global legacy as a pioneer of both military and civilian aviation. He gave his aircrafts Russian names, showing his political and cultural loyalty to mainstream imperial Russian culture.

By the age of just 23, Igor Sikorsky had already become a leading pioneer in Russian aviation and a widely recognised figure. On September 1st, 1913, his multi-engine aircraft *Russki Vityaz* was featured at a major military aviation exhibition, where he was awarded a gold cigarette case for his innovation.

Igor continued his aeronautical research and named his new four-engine aircraft, the *Ilya Muromets* (C-21), after the legendary hero of East Slavic epics whose remains are said to rest at Kyiv's Pechersk Lavra. In June 1914, the *Ilya Muromets* completed a pioneering round trip between St. Petersburg and Kyiv, covering 2,000 kilometres in approximately 14 hours and 40 minutes. Originally designed as a luxury passenger aircraft, the outbreak of World War I prompted its conversion into a military bomber — one of the first of its kind. The aircraft's four engines were reinforced with metal armour, and it was equipped to carry bombs and defensive weaponry. Although the exact number is debated, around 85 units of the *Ilya Muromets* were produced. One legendary account describes how, during a flight, an engine caught fire and a crew member crawled out along the wing midair to extinguish the flames—an almost unbelievable feat that underscored the bravery of its pilots and the rugged durability of Sikorsky's design.

The *Ilya Muromets* was highly valued by the Russian Imperial Government, and in recognition of his achievements, Igor Sikorsky was awarded a financial prize of 75,000 rubles in 1913—a staggering amount at the time, given that the average monthly wage for a worker was around 22.5 rubles. Sikorsky reinvested most of the reward into his ongoing aeronautical research but also purchased a house in the suburbs of Kyiv. That same year, at the age of just 25, he was awarded the prestigious Order of St. Vladimir, Fourth Class—an honour rarely bestowed at such a young age. His growing public stature even found reflection in the arts: composer Alexander Chernyavsky (1871-1942) dedicated a lively and uplifting march titled *The Aviator* to Sikorsky, celebrating the spirit of flight and its young pioneer.

Sikorsky was not only a brilliant engineer but also a skilled pilot who flew the aircraft he designed himself. During World War I, he was deeply involved in frontline aviation work—repairing damaged planes, upgrading returning aircraft, and overseeing production lines. His combination of technical expertise and managerial talent positioned him to expand the Russo-Baltic Wagon Factory into a full-fledged aircraft manufacturer. However, following the February Revolution of 1917, his contract with the factory expired, and due to his close ties with the imperial family, he was discreetly warned that remaining in Russia could be dangerous. Facing political uncertainty and personal risk, Sikorsky left the country and his family. As a respected figure in international aviation, he was able to secure the necessary documents to emigrate swiftly.

Before the Russian Revolution, Igor Sikorsky had married and fathered a daughter. However, as political tensions grew, differences emerged—his wife began sympathising with revolutionary ideals, leading to their eventual divorce. Igor took custody of their daughter and fled first to Murmansk, where British troops were stationed, and from there travelled through the United Kingdom to France. At the time, the French government, having developed a 1,000-kilogram bomb but lacking a suitable aircraft to deliver it, invited Sikorsky to construct a heavy-duty bomber similar to his *Ilya Muromets*. However, with Germany's retreat and the war ending in November 1918, the project was cancelled before completion.

On February 22nd, 1919, his father Ivan passed away in Kyiv, and Igor, who was in Paris, was unable to return home for the funeral, because of the complicated political situation in Ukraine. His father, Ivan, was buried at the Baikove cemetery in Kyiv and his grave still exists.

At the end of March 1919, Igor Sikorsky left Europe for the United States to pursue his career in aircraft engineering. However, the timing was difficult: the U.S. Air Force was downsizing after World War I, and commercial aviation had not yet developed. To make ends meet, he initially worked as a maths teacher at a school for children of Russian immigrants. Determined not to give up, Sikorsky gathered fellow émigré engineers and founded an aircraft manufacturing company that summer. Unfortunately, the business quickly failed and went bankrupt. Undeterred, he travelled to Washington to seek support from military officials and managed to secure a short-term contract to build aircraft. But financial constraints led to the project's cancellation just a month and a half later. Returning to New York, Sikorsky endured a period of severe hardship, living in near poverty while refusing to abandon his dream.

Then, in February 1923, Igor Sikorsky was finally reunited with his sister Olga and his daughter Tatiana, who were able to join him in the United States. During this period, he also met and fell in love with Elizaveta Semyonova, a fellow émigré from the former Russian Empire. They married in January 1924. This marked a turning point in his life: after years of uncertainty and hardship, he was able to rebuild his personal life—he now had a family, a home, and loved ones by his side. With renewed stability, he was finally able to focus fully on his work. In March 1924, Sikorsky founded the Sikorsky Aircraft Corporation. He began building airplanes on a friend's farm in Long Island, New York. Finances remained tight, and the early days were challenging. During this difficult period, he found solace in the music of Pyotr ~~Ilyich~~ Tchaikovsky (1840–1893), Modest Mussorgsky (1839–1881), and Sergei Rachmaninoff (1873–1943) — composers his mother had loved and played during his childhood. In the fall of 1924, when Rachmaninoff was performing in the U.S., Sikorsky attended one of his concerts and met him afterward to express his admiration. Upon hearing about the young engineer's struggles, Rachmaninoff generously lent Sikorsky the $5,000 he had earned from the concert. Likely sensing Sikorsky's brilliance, he offered the support without hesitation. Years later, when the company became successful, Sikorsky repaid the loan in full — with interest.

The Sikorsky Aircraft Corporation gradually became a stable and successful business, producing aircraft such as the ten-seater *S-38* and the transoceanic 40-seater *S-42*. However, Igor Sikorsky never gave up on his childhood dream of vertical flight. In September 1939, he completed the *VS-300* (also known as the *S-46*), one of the first successful single-rotor helicopters, and personally piloted its maiden flight. This moment marked the true beginning of practical helicopter aviation.

By 1944, Sikorsky helicopters were being used by the U.S. military, and they went on to play a critical role during the Korean War in the early 1950s. In a symbolic gesture of technological diplomacy, U.S. President Dwight D. Eisenhower (1890-1969) presented two Sikorsky helicopters to Soviet leader Nikita Khrushchev (1894–1971) during his 1959 state visit to the United States. However, Soviet authorities, wary of using American technology openly, disassembled the helicopters for study at their national research centres. This reverse engineering effort contributed directly to the development of the Soviet *Mi-4* helicopter. In this sense, Igor Sikorsky—ironically exiled by the Bolsheviks—became an indirect godfather of the Soviet helicopter industry as well.

Sikorsky's helicopters have been continuously improved and modernised over the decades. The *S-58* model remains in use in more than 50 countries around the world, while the Sea King—an anti-submarine warfare helicopter developed from the Sikorsky *S-61*—is still actively employed by the Japanese Self-Defense Forces and several other naval forces globally.

If you look at early photographs of Igor Sikorsky, he appears somewhat sombre—a young man carrying the weight of his ambitions. But in photos from his American years, his expression is transformed: calm, assured, perhaps reflecting the fulfillment he found in both his personal and professional life after immigrating to the United States. In his second marriage to Elizaveta Semyonova, he had four sons, one of whom went on to lead the Sikorsky company, which still operates today in Stratford, Connecticut.

Although Sikorsky was never able to return to his native Kyiv/Kiev, the city has honoured his legacy. In 2005, the Kyiv Polytechnic Institute—where he studied but never graduated—was renamed the *Igor Sikorsky Kyiv Polytechnic Institute*. In this way, Sikorsky remains a presence in his hometown. His life story—marked by perseverance, innovation, and an unshakable dream of flight—continues to inspire new generations of young people.

Ukrainian Dreams on the Pacific Rim
Ivan Svit's Far Eastern Mission
(27.04.1897-08.03.1989)

Although Ukrainian-Japanese relations are often overshadowed by broader Russian-Japanese ties, many direct and indirect interactions between Ukraine and Japan date back to the Meiji period. Around 1892-1893, Masutaro Konishi (1869-1948), a Japanese student at the Kyiv Theological Seminary (today's National University of Kyiv-Mohyla Academy), corresponded with Leo Tolstoy (1828-1910) and translated his works into Japanese. Senuma Kakusaburo (1868-1910), a fellow Japanese student and Orthodox Christian who was also studying in Kyiv. Kakusaburo's future wife, Senuma Kayo (1875-1915), would go on to translate many works of Russian literature into Japanese.

Several other figures of Ukrainian origin played significant roles in Japan, although they were often labelled simply as "Russian." For instance, Iosif Goshkevich (1814-1875), the first Imperial Russian consul in Japan, had Belarusian and Ukrainian roots. Vasyl Eroshenko (1890-1952), a blind Ukrainian poet and thinker, published a collection of his writings in Japan with the support of the Nakamuraya company in Shinjuku. Another Ukrainian, Lev (Leo) Mechnikov (1838-1888), was an anarchist intellectual who introduced anarchist thought to Japanese circles.

During the Russian Civil War, Boris Voblyy (02.08.1883 – 1970s?), a Ukrainian émigré, became the first Ukrainian consul and representative of the Ukrainian People's Republic to Japan based in the port city of Tsuruga. Around the same time, Oleksandr Kletny (1891 – 1956), a student at the Kyiv Institute of Finance and Commerce, went to study in Tokyo. His collection of Japanese medicinal herbs is still preserved at the M.G. Kholodny Institute of Botany of the National Academy of Sciences of Ukraine.

In the 20th-century, Ukrainians continued to play key roles in Soviet-Japanese relations. General Kuzma Derevyanko (1904-

1954), who signed Japan's surrender documents on behalf of the Soviet Union at the end of World War II, was also Ukrainian. These cases illustrate how many figures who are typically regarded as "Russian" in Japan came from Ukraine, reflecting deeper and more complex ties between the two nations than is often acknowledged.

After the abolition of serfdom, the Russian Imperial government encouraged migration to the Far East as part of its broader development strategy. Promised generous plots of land and free transportation for entire families, many Ukrainian peasants seized the opportunity. By the early 20th-century, roughly one million Ukrainians had settled in the Russian Far East—out of a regional population of around 15 million. Just before the 1917 Revolution, Ukrainians made up an estimated 70 to 80 percent of the population in some areas.

For these settlers, the Revolution of 1917 was not just about class struggle—it was about national self-determination. In the years that followed, Ukrainians in the Far East and Northeast Asia founded newspapers, organised national cultural clubs, and convened four regional congresses. These gatherings culminated in the drafting of a constitution and plans to establish an autonomous Ukrainian political entity in the region known as *Zelenyi Klyn*, or "Green Ukraine."

During the period of foreign intervention in the Russian Far East and following Japan's occupation of Manchuria, many Ukrainians who aspired to national independence cooperated with Japanese authorities in efforts to establish an autonomous Ukrainian region in the Far East—known as "Green Ukraine" (*Zelenyi Klyn*). In the interwar years, Japan took an active interest in the Ukrainian question. Japanese embassies in China and Germany maintained staff specifically tasked with monitoring

Ukrainian émigrés, collecting intelligence on their activities, political aspirations, and historical background.

By the early 1920s, there were an estimated 750,000 to 1,000,000 people from the former Russian Empire living in the Far East, many of whom were categorised broadly as "Russian." However, a significant portion—especially in cities like Harbin— were of Ukrainian origin. Of the roughly 25,000 "Russians" living in Harbin in the early 1920s, nearly half were Ukrainians.

When Japan occupied Manchuria, it introduced a new ideological framework centered on the concept of the "harmonious coexistence" of different nationalities. In this context, Japanese authorities closely monitored the various ethnic communities living in the region, including Ukrainians. In 1935-36, Japan's Ministry of Foreign Affairs published an extensive report titled *The Political Situation in East Asia*[21], with over 30 pages devoted specifically to analysing the Ukrainian population in Manchuria. This demonstrates that, even when Ukrainian state didn't existed, the Japanese government recognised Ukrainians as a distinct group from Russians.

Following the forced closure of the Japanese consulate in Odesa/Odessa by the Soviet government in September 1937, Manchuria became one of the few places where Japanese diplomats could continue observing Ukrainians in detail. There were even speculative, though unsubstantiated, rumours about the possible opening of a Japanese consulate in Lviv (then Lemberg) in Western Ukraine. In addition to this mid-1930s focus, earlier Japanese diplomatic reports from the period of the Siberian Intervention also documented the Ukrainian national movement in the Russian Far East.

In January 2018, I discovered a typescript in an American archive titled *A Short History of the Ukrainian Movement in Asia*[22], written by Ukrainian journalist, historian, and political activist Ivan Svit. The manuscript, which had never been published

---

21 Tōa seijō (*The Political Situation in East Asia*). Manchukuo Ministry of Foreign Affairs, ed. 1936. "Ukuraina undō gaiken" (*An Overview of the Ukrainian Movement*). *Shinto* 5: 39–72.
22 Svit, Ivan. Skorochena Istoriya Ukrainskogo Rukhu na Dalekomu Skhodi (Asia), written 1938, first published in Olga Khomenko, Dalekoskhidna Odisseia Ivana Svita (Kyiv: Laurus, 2021), 208–410.

before, offers a detailed account of Ukrainian migration to the Russian Far East and Northeast Asia, and traces the emergence of a distinct national movement in the region. Svit spent nearly three decades in the Far East and Asia, witnessing firsthand the Russian Revolution, Japanese intervention, the occupation of Manchuria, and the final years of World War II in the Pacific. His work documents not only the social and cultural life of Ukrainian settlers, particularly farmers, but also the evolution of a political vision: the creation of an autonomous Ukrainian entity called *Zelenyi Klyn* (or "Green Wedge") named for the shape and dense forests of the Ukrainian-populated region. The book was completed on a typewriter in Harbin in January 1938, but never found a publisher and remained in an archive in the United States for decades.

While recently in Ukraine considerable attention has been paid through research and materials in the media to the Ukrainian diaspora in the United States, Canada, Australia, and Argentina; the Ukrainian diaspora in East Asia has gone largely unnoticed and nearly forgotten. This diaspora was also very different from the others, because it almost vanished from Asia after World War II and in the Russian Far East for political reasons stopped identifying itself with Ukraine. In this context, Svit's manuscript is a rare prime source for the history of Ukrainian diaspora in Asia. After World War II and his immigration to the United States, Ivan Svit published another book in Ukrainian called, *Ukrainian-Japanese Relations, 1903–1945: A Historical Survey and Observations*[23]. This 1972 book tells the story of the Ukrainian movement from a global perspective.

The life of Ivan Svit itself reflects the very essence of the history of Ukrainian movement in Asia. Ivan was born on April the 27th, 1897, in Kupiansk, Kharkiv region, Ukraine. His birth name was Ivan Svitlanov. He studied at Kharkiv Theological School, but lost interest in religion and entered the Mathematics Department of the Physics Faculty of Kharkiv University. He was not able to

---

23 Svit, Ivan. Ukrainsko-iaponski vzaiemyny 1903–1945 (Istorychnyi ohliad ta sposterezhennia). New York: Ukrainske Istorychne Tovarystvo, 1972.

finish university because of the Russian revolution and World War I. In early 1918, he decided to go to the United States and chose the longest route to do it—he went to Vladivostok, where his uncle served as a priest in the Far East. Ivan came to Vladivostok in the spring of 1918 when the Ukrainian national movement was forming, holding four congresses of Ukrainians in the Far East and the first local newspaper in Ukrainian, *Ukrainians of Zelenyi Klyn*, started to be published. Later, another Ukrainian language media called *Shyre Slovo* (An Honest Word) was published. After moving to Vladivostok Ivan worked as a journalist at several newspapers, at a Ukrainian news agency, and at the navy headquarters. Watching the Ukrainian national movement emerging he also shortened his last name to sound more Ukrainian and began publishing under the pen name Ivan Svit (in Ukrainian *svit* means "world").

Following the four Universals of the Ukrainian Central Council in Kyiv, four All-Ukrainian Far Eastern Congresses were held in 1917-18 and aimed to create an independent Ukrainian political entity called Green Ukraine. At the fourth Congress, held at the end of October and beginning of November 1918, "The Ukrainians declaration to the People of the World" and a "Constitution of Green Ukraine" was developed. Ivan Svit witnessed and recorded as a journalist, and later an historian, all the events taking place during this period. It is only natural that his national identity and consciousness became a political choice and thereby became even firmer.

In 1922, when the Soviet regime finally consolidated control over the Russian Far East—after nearly five years of civil war and a shifting patchwork of governments—Ivan Svit, like many of his fellow Ukrainians, was forced to flee to Harbin under threat of arrest by the Bolsheviks. While the Far Eastern Republic (April 1920 to November 1922), a Soviet-aligned buffer state, had technically existed since 1920, its authority was weak and transitional, and by late 1922 it was fully absorbed into the USSR.

Harbin, about 640 kilometres from Vladivostok, became a shelter for displaced Ukrainians. Since 1900, many specialists from the Russian Empire—particularly railway engineers and administrators—had moved to the region to build and run the Chinese Eastern Railway. Ukrainians were well represented, and Harbin soon developed a vibrant community with Ukrainian clubs, newspapers, and a strong intellectual presence. Among those who helped shape this environment was General Dmitry Horvat (1859-1937), originally from Kremenchuk in the Poltava region, who oversaw the railway and employed many Ukrainian experts.

Ivan Svit, a native of Kupyansk in the Kharkiv region, was accustomed to switching between Ukrainian—spoken at home—and Russian—used in schools and cities like Kharkiv—so he never felt entirely out of place in Harbin's multilingual, multiethnic environment. After moving to Harbin, Svit became an important member of the Ukrainian community, writing and editing newspapers and magazines in the city. In his publications and editorial materials, he reflected the history of Ukrainian movement in the region, as well as the situation in Soviet Ukraine including the 1932—33 famine, oppression and murder of intellectuals under the Stalin regime, and the absence of freedom. He finished the manuscript of the *Short History of the Ukrainian Movement in the Far East (Asia)* in January 1938[24], exactly on the 20th anniversary of the founding of the short-lived Ukrainian People's Republic (UPR). As the number of witnesses to the history of the Ukrainian movement in the Far East dwindled, Svit undoubtedly wanted the efforts of many activists to be remembered in this manuscript.

According to Ivan Svit, Ukrainians in Asia were not mere guests, transit migrants or refugees, but were settlers who created life and culture and wanted to have their own life on their own land, living by their own order.

Svit writes in an accessible language, that although Ukraine was part of the Russian Empire, the Far East was developed through efforts of Ukrainian farmers, therefore it is still considered outer Ukraine with many green forests. Ukrainian farmers moved to the Far East, cleared the land, and created a way of life

---

24 Svit, Skorochena Istoriya Ukrainskogo Rukhu, in Khomenko, Dalekoskhidna Odisseia.

based on Ukrainian traditions and customs learned from their grandfathers and grandmothers. A new Ukrainian colony slowly formed, and during the Ukrainian independence movement of Green Ukraine was of utmost importance. In the process of developing 1917-1922 national consciousness, theatre performances, choral groups, Ukrainian language schools, and Ukrainian clubs were established. There was also the influence of Ukrainian military men representing different armies stationed in the Far East during World War I. And just before the revolution of 1917, Ukrainians in the Far East gained enough strength to shift their emphasis from cultural to political activities.

In the new environment of China, Svit played various roles. He was a journalist, social activist, historian, businessman, and philatelist. He was also interested in stamps and operated as a dealer from the time he moved to Harbin.

In the late 1930s, there were between 50,000 and 100,000 Ukrainians living in China, mostly concentrated in the Harbin and Shanghai area. Many people from the Russian Empire had moved from the Far East, and they were all called "White Russians," regardless of them being Jews, Georgians, Tatars, and other ethnic groups. Few activists like Ivan Svit flew to Manchuria, they collaborated with established Ukrainians and together they made efforts to unite the Ukrainian community under the same language, culture, religion, social and cultural events, and organisations. In Harbin, there were Ukrainian Orthodox churches, school, clubs, a publishing house, and newspapers.

The Ukrainian Orthodox Church acquired land in Harbin in the late 1910s, and after a year of collecting donations from Ukrainian fellows, built the independent building in 1930 and called it the *Church of the Holy Protection of the Mother of God*. That church still stands in Harbin. Old postcards may describe it as the *Russian Church* in English, however, in Japanese it is called the *Ukrainian Cathedral*. The first priest of the church was Prokip Gordzievski followed by Ivan Svit's uncle, Mykola (Nikolai) Trufanov, who served as head priest from 1924 to 1944. So, Ivan Svit moved to Harbin together with or following his maternal uncle.

When Manchukuo was established in 1932, backed by Japanese military power, there were 11,000 Ukrainians living in the city, and they gathered around the cultural centre of Ukrainian House. Svit was also a member of the Management Board of the Ukrainian Association and had connections with ex-officials from the independent Ukrainian government in Europe.

With the establishment of Manchukuo, promoting racial and ethnic harmony, the Ukrainian diaspora hoped for an improvement in its social status. Svit leveraged his connections with Japanese officers from his time in the Far East to promote Ukrainian interests. With the help of Kazumasa Horie, who was posted in Manchuria to work at the intelligence department of the South Manchuria Railway Company *(Mantetsu johobu)* and he had sympathy for the Ukrainian diaspora in Manchuria. This sympathy was inspired by his family circumstances—he had married a Ukrainian woman named Anastasia since his dispatch to Vladivostok during the Allied intervention in the Russian Civil War. His boss, former diplomat and Russianist Furusawa Kokichi, granted permission for publication of the trilingual newspaper *The Manchurian Herald* from September of 1932 to August of 1937. The paper supported oppressed ethnic groups like Tatars, Poles, and Georgians. The Japanese state carefully observed different minority groups in the region working to create a non-national entity where all coexisted harmoniously, whilst Ukrainians sought to establish an independent Ukrainian multinational political entity in the Far East. This dynamic involved both governmental and non-governmental Japanese agents, many of whom were influenced by modernity, facilitated by the translation of Russian intellectual ideas into Japanese society during the early 20th-century [25].

The newspaper not only served the Ukrainian community but also addressed broader minority issues, reflecting Svit's inclu-

---

[25] Sho Konishi, Anarchist Modernity: Cooperatism and Japanese-Russian Intellectual Relations in Modern Japan (Harvard University Asia Centre, 2013).

sive vision. The initial circulation was 1500 copies, and it was published for five years until the end of the summer of 1937 when Japanese authorities withdrew permission for publication. Two hundred issues were published, containing articles not only from local Manchurian residents who were practicing journalism, but also correspondents from Lviv, Berlin, and New York, reflecting Ivan Svit's global mind and strong international network. It was also sold not only in Manchuria and China, but also in Japan and other countries. From the beginning, the newspaper was based on a multilingual ideology and considered the oppressed peoples, not only Ukrainians, but also Tatars, Poles, and Georgians[26].

Initially, he received financial support from Ivan Shevchenko, a wealthy Ukrainian businessman, but later he established personal contacts with Japanese government officials, and it appears he also had the support of the Japanese military. Svit had also thought of publishing a similar weekly newspaper in Japanese, but this plan unfortunately was not realised.

First issue of The Manchurian Herald, 5 August 1932, reporting that Japan is recognising the state of Manchukuo

---

26 Mandzurskiy Vistnyk 1932: 1, 6

Svit was a connector, uniting many people and delivering several valuable projects. With the support of Stepan Levynskyi, the economic attaché at the Polish consulate, he managed to publish a map of the Far East called "Green Ukraine."

On March 19, 1937, a significant milestone was achieved with the publication of a colour map of the territory of "Green Ukraine." This initiative was led by M. Stankevich, working at the railway and O. Istomin, a geodesist. Their efforts were supported by Kazumasa Horie's technical expertise, financial support by Stepan Levynskyi, Ukrainian writer and diplomat, working in the Polish consulate economical section, and the ongoing coordination and patronage of Ivan Svit. A total of 1,100 copies were published in Ukrainian[27].

The publication faced numerous obstacles, particularly from the Soviet consulate in Harbin, which expressed dissatisfaction over the depiction of a non-existent country on the map. The consulate attempted to halt the publication, but Japanese authorities permitted it on the condition that the Soviet Union's territory was accurately shown, and "Green Ukraine" was included in brackets[28].

The publication of this map was more than a cartographic endeavour; it was a political statement. It aimed to illustrate the extent of the "Green Wedge" and establish the geographical name "Green Ukraine" (Mapa, 1937). This effort symbolised the aspiration to create a country for Ukrainian immigrants in the Far East, envisioning a unique state from the Amur River to the Pacific coast.

The map was distributed not only in Manchuria but also internationally, available for purchase in the USA, Poland, and Japan at reasonable prices. It depicted the territories of "Green Ukraine," Manchukuo, China, Korea, Outer Mongolia, and the Japanese archipelago; highlighting lowlands, highlands, remote roads, radio stations, railways (including those under construc-

---

27 Chornomaz, V., ed. Ukrainci v Kytai: entsyklopedychnyi dovidnyk [Ukrainians in China: Encyclopedic Reference]. Odesa: Helvetyka, 2021: 163.
28 Svit 1972: 217

tion), airports, coal mines, and lumber centres. Boundaries at various administrative levels were drawn, and towns and villages were identified. *The Manchurian Herald* described it as an "ethnographic map showing the current situation in various ways," including all tractor stations and forestry centres under Communist control[29].

Ivan Svit also played a pivotal role in coordinating and editing the publication of the *Ukrainian-Japanese Dictionary*, a project that began in Harbin around 1938-39, with editing commencing in 1941. The dictionary was ultimately published in 1944 by orientalists Anatoly Dibrova and Vasyl Odynets. This effort received financial backing from Petro Horowyi's inheritance, a Ukrainian businessman who had fled to Harbin after being convicted in January of 1924 Chita Trial of Ukrainian activists[30].

The dictionary's content included Ukrainian words followed by Russian translations and Japanese meanings in kanji, along with Roman alphabet pronunciations (Ukrainian-Japanese Dictionary, 1944). It featured foreign words in katakana, synonyms for some entries, and Russian terms to aid Japanese military personnel familiar with Russian. Unlike traditional Polivanov Japanese transcriptions used in Russian, the dictionary used a unique method devised by Anatoly Dibrova, which more accurately reflected Japanese sounds and Ukrainian phonetics. The dictionary, published during World War II, underscored the transnational presence of Ukrainians and their desire for self-determination with a circulation of several thousand copies and 11,000 entries and 270 pages. According to Nakai Kazuo, publication was apparently supported by the Japanese military or the Manchurian Railway. Since among the Far East's population of 2,700,000 people, 1,250,000 were Ukrainians (110,000 Russians), Japan felt the importance of the Ukrainian language and saw the significance of speaking to them in their native language. Perhaps,

---

29 Mandzurskiy Vistnyk, 21.03.1937.
30 Ivan Svit, *Ukrainsko-iaponski vzaiemyny 1903–1945 (Istorychnyi ohliad ta sposterezhennia)* (New York: Ukrainske Istorychne Tovarystvo, 1972), 295–96.

the Japanese military intended to directly manipulate the Ukrainians living in Manchuria[31].

Meantime, there were many Ukrainians living in Shanghai, necessitating a Ukrainian bank and a Ukrainian school. In the summer of 1941, when the war between Nazi Germany and the Soviet Union broke out, Ivan Svit moved to Shanghai and relocated his stamp shop there to support himself and Maria Grigor (Maria Svit), a Ukrainian theatre actress whom he had married in Harbin. He was also one of the main figures of the Ukrainian community in Shanghai. He had long and difficult negotiations with the Shanghai authorities to get the attention of the international community but was able to publish a fortnightly newspaper called *The Call of the Ukraine* in English instead of Ukrainian. He kept writing about wartime life and conditions in his native Ukraine in the newspaper and also made short new programmes for radio during 1941 to 1943. Meanwhile, he also worked as a journalist, in the fortnightly Ukrainian-language newspaper called *The Ukrainian Voice. Far Eastern Review*, where he wrote about people's lives in Shanghai and Ukraine in addition to posting the political and economic news. It seems that prewar activities of most of the Ukrainian community in Shanghai compared to Harbin were more cultural rather than political. There were many theatrical and dance performances, as well as exhibitions.

Ukrainians in Shanghai had mixed feelings about the USSR. Many had disliked the Soviet Union ever since its formation and after learning that some of their fellows who returned to the USSR were immediately prosecuted. However, after Germany's invasion of the Soviet Union many emigrants who had participated in World War I became sympathetic to the USSR. After reading newspaper articles, others cheered Germany for allowing education and masses to be conducted in Ukraine whilst the Germans occupied Ukrainian territories. Ukrainians moved to Asia because of diverse political, ideological, and economic reasons, therefore their ways of thinking also varied greatly.

---

31 Kazuo Nakai, *Ukraine in America, and Japan, Mado* (Window), no. 45 (1983): 14–19, Nauka.

When the war ended, Svit became one of the key figures in charge of the Ukrainian association responsible for Ukrainians' exodus from China. The primary documents I saw in New York gave a glimpse of what it was like. He was involved in negotiations with the Chinese authorities, the Red Cross, and the International Refugee Organisation, explaining that Ukrainians in Shanghai were nether Russians or Soviet citizens, therefore requesting that they be allowed to leave China. He helped to reregister the community, collecting the records and photographs for that new registration from Ukrainian refugees in China to obtain the necessary stateless documents and permits. The documents reveal Ivan's meticulous nature. People had to complete an application form with their name, age, religion, profession, social status back in Ukraine, as well as the year they arrived in China and also to Shanghai in particular. However, some senior members could not remember their place or date of birth. Therefore, upon the final submission of the papers, Svit had to provide many explanations to receive the permits for each Ukrainian to leave China. Some of the Russian community in Shanghai returned to the USSR. However, 198 adults and 71 children through Svit's efforts and with the cooperation of the US Navy, were able to move first to the Philippines and then emigrate to Argentina, the United States, and Australia.

Svit himself was initially permitted to emigrate to the United States because his wife Maria had relatives living in Alaska. Yet someone reported him for collaboration with the Japanese, which led to the revocation of his visa. In the end, with the strong support of the Ukrainian community in the United States who went to the media and congress, in April 1949, he moved with his wife to Taiwan and from there to Alaska. Through lecturing and moving through many Canadian cities he finally reached New York. Considering that some Ukrainians were left in China until around 1952 or 1953 without visas and any chances to emigrate later being deported to the USSR and killed, Svit was indeed fortunate.

In the United States, he was known as John V. Svit and again was an active member of the Ukrainian community. He also interacted with many intellectuals and cultural figures, such as Leontiy Turkevych (1876–1965), the Metropolitan of the North American Diocese of the Russian Orthodox Church in the USA, who was originally from Volhynia region of Ukraine; and with John of Shanghai (Mykhailo Maksymovych) (1896–1966), a the Bishop of the Russian Orthodox Church Outside Russia, who similarly to Svit was born in Kharkiv region and with whom Svit got acquainted during his time in Shanghai[32]. Because he did not have a university diploma, in the USA, Ivan Svit ended up in different low paid jobs and continued to write at night. During the day he worked at the YMCA to make ends meet, and at night he studied and wrote at home or at the New York Public Library.

His research and writing in the USA, especially in the Ukrainian community, produced even greater results in later years. Being an immigrant himself, Svit wrote and spoke frequently about Ukrainian movements in Asia. It was an unknown subject for many people. Because of his efforts he brought the Ukrainian experience in Asia to history. Ukrainian experience of migration and history of Ukrainian migration, previously limited to the USA, Canada, and Europe, was reimagined as a global phenomenon.

Thanks to his family background and his earlier studies at theological school at a young age, after moving to New York he became interested in the history of Ukrainians involved in popularisation of Orthodoxy in the United States. Intrigued by the life of Agapiy Goncharenko (1832–1916), the first Ukrainian immigrant and Orthodox priest, Ivan Svit did a lot of research and wrote several research papers. He also became a member of *The Ukrainian Academy of Arts and Sciences in the U.S.A* (UVAN), which was founded by exiled intellectuals first in Germany and then moved to the USA. He attempted to publish a book on a history of Ukrainian migration in the Far East, but this was never completed.

He was also a member of the Ukrainian Historical Society in the USA and was also involved in the establishment of the journal *The*

---

32 According to Ivan Svit's letter to Stanislav Kulchytskyi of July 14, 1963, UVAN.

Ukrainian Historian. He also became president of the Ukrainian Philatelic and Numismatic Society of America and published the society's journal *Ukrainian Philatelist* in Ukrainian from 1961 to 1974. Remembering those who once fought together for Ukrainian independence in the Far East, Svit published also in Ukrainian *The Trial of the Ukrainians in China (1923-1924)* through a London publisher in 1964.

The most notable book of his life in the U.S. is the *Ukrainian-Japanese Relations, 1903–1945: A Historical Survey and Observations*, published in New York in 1972. To date, this is one of few books written on the history of diplomatic and cultural relations between Japan and Ukraine. It is a massive book consisting of 14 chapters and 371 pages in total. The first chapter is called *A General Survey of Japanese History, with an Evaluation and Orientation of Japanese Policy*, covering Japan's interest in ethnic issues in Europe, political confrontations in the Far East after World War I, the founding of Manchukuo and the Ukrainian community from its establishment to the cessation of activities, and the lives of Ukrainians at the time and their postwar evacuation. The book can be interpreted as both a memoir as well as a primary historical source.

Until I visited the archives in New York, I had presumed that Svit spoke and wrote in Japanese. However, when I checked his personal papers, I could not find even a single note written in Japanese characters. If he could speak Japanese, he would certainly have left something somewhere within his notes. Or maybe the papers were carefully selected before he donated them to the archive. Or perhaps he could speak but could not write in Japanese. This will remain a mystery, although most of the Japanese elite bureaucrats and military in Manchuria were able to speak Russian, because they were educated in the department of Russian language in Tokyo, so Svit probably had no issues with communication. On the other hand, if you read the preface to the *Ukrainian-Japanese Relations, 1903–1945: A Historical Survey and Observations*, you will understand that he asked others to assist him with the translation of Japanese names and documents. That was all contributed by other people. In any case, even without sufficient language skills, he had a vision and the power to move people; to collaborate toward creating something bigger. The newspaper project, the map, and the dictionary are all speaking for themselves.

Ivan Svit embodied a deeply rooted and consciously chosen Ukrainian identity shaped by revolution, exile, and cultural activism. Born in Kupiansk, Kharkiv region, he embraced Ukrainian language and national consciousness while witnessing the Ukrainian movement in the Russian Far East, known as "Green Ukraine" (Zelenyi Klyn). He shortened his surname from Svitlanov to the more Ukrainian "Svit" and dedicated his life to documenting and promoting the Ukrainian political and cultural presence in Asia. Through his work as a journalist, editor, and historian in Harbin and Shanghai, he championed the idea of Ukrainian autonomy, founded Ukrainian-language publications, co-organised the publication of a Ukrainian-Japanese dictionary, and produced a political map of "Green Ukraine." Even in exile, Svit remained committed to the Ukrainian cause, culminating in his 1972 book *Ukrainian-Japanese Relations, 1903–1945: A Historical Survey and Observations* — a pioneering work that positioned Ukraine as a distinct actor in international affairs. His life and legacy reflect a transnational form of Ukrainian patriotism that transcended borders and sought global recognition for Ukraine's historical and cultural identity.

Across Continents, Toward Japan
The Life of Stepan Levynskyi/Stefan Lewinski (1897-1946)

The blind poet Vasil Eroshenko (1890-1952) was perhaps the only Ukrainian writer to write about Japanese themes and people actually in the Japanese language. During the 19th and early 20th centuries, very few Ukrainians studied Japanese professionally or left behind any literary work on Japan. However, there is one remarkable exception — a writer who remains largely forgotten today. His name was Stepan Levynskyi (or Stefan Lewinski in Polish), a man known for his sharp wit and charming smile. Born in 1897 in Lviv, he was the son of the renowned architect Ivan Levynskyi (also registered as Jan Lewinski in Polish records). His father played a major role in shaping Ukrainian modernist architecture, with many of his buildings still standing in Lviv. Ivan also founded a tile factory that produced not only roof and wall tiles and ceramic stoves, but also uniquely designed vases and flowerpots featuring distinct Ukrainian motifs.

Stephan Levynskyi grew up in an environment filled with books, architectural drawings, and ornamental designs. After graduating from the chemistry department of the Lviv Polytechnic Institute, he travelled to France in 1922 to continue his studies at the Paris Institute of Technology. He then moved to Antwerp to attend the newly established Colonial University of Belgium, which trained personnel for the Belgian colonies in Congo and Ruanda-Urundi. Although he earned an engineering qualification, Levynskyi had long been fascinated by Japan. Instead of pursuing a colonial career in Africa, he returned to France and enrolled at the *National Institute of Languages and Oriental Civilization* (INALCO), founded in 1669, to study Japanese. In 1929, he was granted residence at the Maison du Japon ("Japanese House"), a dormitory for Japanese students within the newly established Cité Internationale Universitaire de Paris — a campus conceived after World War I to foster peace and international understanding. There, he formed deep connections with Japanese students; relationships that would shape his thinking and future work. *The Japanese House* was among the first national pavilions constructed at the Cité, reflecting Japan's early commitment to international education and cultural exchange.

After graduating from the National Institute of Languages and Oriental Civilisation, Stepan Levynskyi received a recommendation from the institute's president for a teaching position as a French instructor at a school in Fukuoka, Japan. However, due to poor health, he temporarily returned to his family home in Western Ukraine. While recuperating at a sanatorium in Vorokhta in the Carpathian Mountains, he wrote a book titled *Letters from the Japanese House*[33], reflecting on his year at the Maison du Japon and the friendships he formed there. The book was serialised in the prominent Western Ukrainian daily *Dilo* ("Business") between 1931 and 1932. In 1933, he was awarded the Writers and Journalists Association Prize for this work.

Levynskyi visited the Japanese Embassy in Paris several times to meet with diplomat Mr. Yanai. Fortunately, I was able to locate an introductory letter written by Mr. Yanai to the foundation that managed the Maison du Japon — an institution Levynskyi fondly describes in his writings. For Stepan, being accepted into the Maison du Japon felt like a dream come true: it brought him closer to Japan, the distant and enigmatic country he had long admired.

---

33 Levynskyi, S. Vid Vezuviia do piskiv Sakhary. Z yaponskoho domu. Skhid i Zakhid. Lviv: LA Piramida, 2018.

The Maison du Japon, located near Parc Montsouris, was often described as a "Little Japan" in Paris. It is a modernist building of glass and concrete designed by French architect Pierre Sardou (1873-1952) and funded by Jirohachi Satsuma (1863-1943), a wealthy Japanese merchant and philanthropist from the Kobe area who sponsored international cultural initiatives, including funding the construction of the Maison du Japon in Paris and helped foster stronger ties between Japan and France in education and the arts. Inside the residence were two striking murals—*The Arrival of Westerners in Japan* and *The Horses*—painted by the renowned Japanese artist Tsuguharu Fujita (1886-1968), who gained fame in Paris as part of the early 20th-century avant-garde scene, also known for blending Japanese aesthetics with Western techniques.

Everything was new to Stepan in that dormitory in Paris. It was his first time living with Japanese people and he was the only foreigner there. He made many discoveries about their lifestyle, customs, sense of beauty, and mindset. In his writings, Levynskyi mentions several fellow male residents: Shokichi, an economics student from Tokyo; Mizuno, a medical student; Maekawa, an architecture graduate; Kimura, a chemist; Ito, a high school teacher; Matsui, a philosophy student with the appearance of a monk; and Sugimoto, a mathematician. Although Stepan had studied *keigo* (the honorific form of the Japanese language) at school, he initially struggled to understand everyday conversations. But the longer he lived with his Japanese peers, the more his language skills improved. I investigated that the architecture student Maekawa is Maekawa Kunio (1905-1986). He later became a prominent architect and introduced modernist architecture to Japan. After studying with Le Corbusier, he became known for his influential public buildings like Tokyo Metropolitan Art Museum (1959) in Ueno Park, National Museum of Modern Art in Kyoto (1963) and Saitama Cultural Centre (1966). Maekawa also mentored the next generation of prominent Japanese architects, including Kenzo Tange (1913-2005)[34], helping to lay the foundation for Japan's global reputation in architecture.

One of the central themes in *Letters from the Japanese House* is the relationship between men and women. A Japanese man meets a Western woman for the first time, becomes her friend, and eventually falls in love. The protagonist sometimes is a fictionalised version of Levinskyi himself. The book introduces several women: an Englishwoman who is emotionally and financially independent; a Russian woman shaped by hardship and somewhat self-centred in her interactions with men; a spirited and slightly wild Filipino woman; and a French cabaret dancer who is sexually liberated and open in her lifestyle. Through these characters, the book explores how the Japanese protagonists, unfamiliar with such women, gradually adapt and reflect on their feelings.

Paris in 1928-1929 was experiencing a glamorous cultural renaissance — Josephine Baker (1906-1975) was enchanting audiences with the Charleston, while surrealist Man Ray (1890-1976) captured iconic photographs of celebrities. The city was a magnet for admirers from around the world. For Stepan, coming from the small and close-knit city of Lviv and the conservative atmosphere of Antwerp, Paris felt like a personal liberation. Living in the specially designed "Little Japan" within Paris — the Maison du Japon — must have added a unique layer to that experience.

At the time, most of the Japanese visitors in Paris were male students on short educational stays. Japanese women were rare in the city, with perhaps the only notable exception being a ballerina named Oma, who performed at the Théâtre Femina. Stepan saw her on stage and wrote about her striking beauty and dance style, which blended Japanese and Western traditions. He noted her shy

---

34 Kenzo Tange (1913-2005) was a pioneering Japanese architect whose work bridged traditional Japanese design with modernist architecture. A recipient of the 1987 Pritzker Architecture Prize, his most notable projects include the Hiroshima Peace Memorial Park (1949-1956), St. Mary's Cathedral in Tokyo (1964), the Yoyogi National Gymnasium built for the 1964 Tokyo Olympics and Tokyo Metropolitan Government Building (1991). Tange's influence extended globally, shaping postwar architecture across Asia, Europe, and the Middle East.

smile, so different from the self-assured expressions of Western women, and her delicate way of reciting poetry.

Another Japanese woman Stepan wrote about was Michiko, the wife of his friend Sugimoto, who also lived in the dormitory. To spend time with her, Stepan offered to teach her French while walking through the streets of Paris. He wrote that he "admired the secret of Eastern women and tried to solve it." Eventually, unable to contain his emotions, he confessed his feelings—but Michiko simply smiled and ran away. Whether her reaction was due to cultural misunderstanding, limited French, or simply a lack of mutual affection remains unknown.

Levynskyi reflected on his admiration for the kindness and talkativeness of the Japanese people, the delicious food, and the beauty of their tableware. He observed how Japanese women gazed at flowers—long and humbly—as if they were sacred icons in an Orthodox church.

We can observe Stepan's artistic maturation in the way he describes people and experiences. He also painted vivid images of Japanese cuisine, which was still rare and exotic in Europe at the time. Dining for the first time at the well-known Japanese restaurant *Botan-ya*, advertised in a Parisian newspapers back then, he was served *osuimono* (a clear soup) as an appetiser, followed by *sashimi* as the main course. Although raw fish was generally considered unpalatable for foreigners, Stepan found the taste surprisingly enjoyable. "I don't know if any Japanese writer or poet ever wrote about sashimi," he noted, "but it was very tasty and praiseworthy." He went on to reflect: "Miso soup is something Japanese people eat every day, and the children of the Land of the Rising Sun who go abroad miss it deeply and seize every chance to enjoy that delicious bean soup." He was also fascinated by Japanese rice, writing, "Japanese rice has a special secret. They eat it with all their food at the same time." Though there were no rice cookers at the time, he added with admiration, "Asians cook the rice very well."

Moreover, Levynskyi noted that "tea is a special art in the East," observing that it is always drunk without sugar and often in place of water. He described with admiration the traditional dish *ochazuke*, in which tea is poured over leftover rice at the end of a meal, likening its humble beauty to a "last supper." His writing conveys a deep respect for and curiosity about Japanese culinary traditions. He emphasised that such practices, unfamiliar to Westerners, are integral to Japanese etiquette and cultural sensibility. With a touch of irony, he remarked that "seafood from the distant southern seas is served on lovely plates—a rarity for vulgar Westerners who are satisfied with meat and bread." Levynskyi clearly loved Japan and the broader East, but he never romanticised it blindly. Rather than seeing East and West in opposition, he appreciated cultural difference with an open yet critical eye, avoiding the trap of colonial exoticism.

Levynskyi's deep admiration for Asian culture is evident in his reflections: he wrote that he "was looking hard for the Orient in Paris. I felt a heart-stirring longing for something mysterious, and exotic hidden behind their faces, their gestures, their ways of thinking and their words." At a time when France held colonial dominion over large parts of Southeast Asia—dating formally from the 1880s, if not earlier—Asians, including the Japanese, were often viewed through a lens of condescension by French society. Although Japan had asserted itself on the world stage by defeating Russia in 1905 and acquiring former German colonies after World War I, it was still perceived in Europe as a distant, intriguing, and potentially threatening "other." Levynskyi, however, approached Japan from a different vantage point. Born in western Ukraine, a region long shaped by shifting empires—Polish-Lithuanian, Austro-Hungarian, and others—he was unusually receptive to cultural plurality. His fascination with Japan was free from imperial arrogance or exoticising gaze; instead, he embraced it with genuine curiosity and empathy, allowing him to engage with the culture on more equal and human terms.

In his passage titled *Secrets of Asia*, Levynskyi introduces a Japanese man named Akira, a regular visitor to the Maison du Japon. Akira had survived the Great Kanto Earthquake in 1923 at a young age, after which his family relocated from Tokyo to Osaka. At the age of eight, he began working alongside his father in a spinning mill, where he not only came to understand the value of money but also witnessed the harsh realities of social and economic inequality. These early experiences gradually drew him toward leftist ideology, and he eventually took part in strikes at mills and factories. Later, Akira found work as a crew member on a ship and travelled widely, seeking wisdom from various cultures around the world. His journey ultimately brought him to Paris, where he began studying cinematography.

"If it is true that God puts a soul in a body at birth," Levynskyi wrote, "then God must have put into Akira's body a traveller's soul who likes the whole world, every part of it, and can make it his home." This poignant line encapsulates Stepan Levynskyi's admiration for Akira—not merely as a character, but as a symbol of freedom, resilience, and cosmopolitan identity.

Raised in relatively strict conditions in Catholic Lviv, albeit in a wealthy and cultured family, Levynskyi himself had access to international education but lacked the inner liberty he perceived in Akira. In contrast to the more reserved and insular Japanese students who stayed within the Maison du Japon, Akira walked his own path. He had survived the Great Kanto Earthquake, laboured in Osaka's mills, sailed across continents, and arrived in Paris to study cinematography—his journey shaped by hardship and a restless pursuit of knowledge and justice.

This passage shows Stepan Levynskyi's deep emotional and moral alignment with anti-colonial sympathies. In Akira, he saw not only the ideal of a free, globe-trotting spirit but also a comrade in resisting oppression—perhaps a reflection of his own upbringing in a multi-imperial, contested Ukraine. Raised in Catholic Lviv under Polish rule, Levynskyi was acutely aware of national subjugation. That awareness shaped his admiration for people like Akira, who rejected submission and sought justice—even through radical means.

Although Levynskyi does not explicitly endorse Akira's later path of political violence, his writing subtly expresses empathy for those struggling against colonialism. His sympathetic portrayal of Vietnamese students being suppressed by French police further reinforces this. Stepan's voice in *Letters from the Japanese House* reveals a man with both admiration for Asian cultures and a deeper understanding of the power dynamics shaping East–West relations — one who could recognise injustice not as distant or foreign, but as something painfully familiar.

Levynskyi's narrative does not shy away from complexity. When Akira witnessed a riot of Vietnamese students at the Maison de l'Indochine being violently suppressed by white French police, he reportedly felt a moral obligation as a fellow Asian: to "rebel against the oppression of the white people." Although Akira's later turn to terrorism is mentioned, Levynskyi's tone remains empathetic. His portrayal suggests not judgment, but an understanding shaped by his own history — coming from a region long subjected to foreign rule, where national identity had often been denied or suppressed.

In that sense, Levynskyi is not simply recounting Akira's story — he is also processing his own place within a world structured by empire, power, and race. His sympathy toward anti-colonial resistance, his fascination with Japan, and his search for global connection reveal a man with a deep humanist spirit, attuned to injustice in both his homeland and abroad.

In conservative, Catholic Lviv, *Letters from the Japanese House* — with its open reflections on women and interethnic relationships — was criticised for its frank treatment of gender and social dynamics. At the time, such content may have been challenging for readers in what was still a relatively provincial city. Yet reading it today, one is struck not by its controversy but by Stepan Levynskyi's energy, keen observational eye, and vibrant, cheerful spirit that shines through his words.

Prewar Lviv was part of Poland, and so Levynskiy as a Polish citizen was able to secure a position with the Polish diplomatic mission abroad. From 1935 to 1940, he lived and worked in Harbin as an economic attaché and Japanese interpreter at the Polish Consulate. At that time, Harbin had a large Ukrainian population, and Levynskyi actively participated in community life, engaging in translation and publishing efforts aimed at deepening mutual understanding between the Japanese and local Ukrainians. As a government official, Levynskyi enjoyed a better standard of living than many other Ukrainians struggling to get by in Harbin, and he used his position to support various cultural initiatives. Recent research also suggests that he was sent to Harbin by Polish intelligence to involve the Ukrainian diaspora in the Polish political project of Prometheism, which aimed to unite all oppressed nations of the former Russian Empire in order to dismantle the Soviet state. In 1937, he financed the publication of a map of "Green Ukraine", and in 1944, he contributed entries to the first Japanese-Ukrainian dictionary. He also collaborated with Ivan Svit on plans to publish a 30-page Japanese-language periodical every two months—but unfortunately, the project was never realised.

Between 1934 and 1935, Stepan Levynskyi wrote a series of articles on life in Asia for the Ukrainian magazine *Nazustrich* (which means "To Meet" or "Towards Encounter"). A compilation of these writings was later published in two volumes in Ukraine in 2020.

Levynskyi's writing stands out for its vivid style and engaging tone—his descriptions of people and places, as well as his direct dialogue with the reader, makes one feel like a close friend of the author. In his native Western Ukraine, he was widely recognised as an expert on Asian affairs, particularly regarding countries like Morocco, Turkey, Japan, and China, all of which he had travelled to extensively.

In his essay *Minutes of Japan and China*, written during his time in Manchuria, Stepan Levynskyi explores the multifaceted impact of Western culture and fashion on Japanese women, reflecting on how these influences subtly reshape character and identity. He devotes attention to the aesthetics of Japanese poetry—particularly *tanka* and *haiku* [35] —as well as the enduring influence of visual arts, religious beliefs, and philosophical traditions. The essay also reveals Levynskyi's sensitivity to landscape and change, as he documents his impressions of Tokyo, Kyoto, and Nara, observing how each city evolves while retaining traces of its historical soul. Through these reflections, he not only charts

---

35 Tanka is a 31-syllable Japanese poem (5-7-5-7-7), while haiku is a later 17-syllable form (5-7-5) usually focused on nature or seasonal themes

cultural transformation, but also deepens his exploration of the tension between modernity and tradition in East Asia.

Levynskyi also turned his pen toward the everyday lives of Ukrainian settlers in Manchuria. His 1941 essay *Travelling Birds* offers a rare and valuable glimpse into their lifestyles, explored through the story of a hunting trip with a visiting British merchant. Bird hunting, a common leisure activity among the upper-middle class in Manchuria, serves here as both a cultural lens and backdrop. Another notable work, *Maznytsya Daughter's Wedding* (1941), written in Beijing, tells the story of a girl from a Ukrainian family who emigrated to Manchuria, fell in love with a Japanese man, and sought her father's blessing for marriage. The story delicately captures the emotional tension of a father caught between his traditional background and the changing world around him—himself a war-displaced exile, now witnessing his daughter bridge cultures through love. These poignant stories were published posthumously in the March 8th, 1952 edition of *Svoboda*, a Ukrainian-language newspaper in the United States, thanks to the efforts of Ivan Svit.

Before heading to Manchuria for his diplomatic and cultural work, Stepan Levynskyi published several travelogues that reflected his expanding global perspective. In 1926, he wrote *From Vesuvius to the Sahara*, a vivid account of his journey from Italy to Africa. Later, in 1934, he published *Turkey: East and West*, documenting his impressions of a country straddling two civilisations. Beyond travel writing, Levynskyi also made pioneering contributions to cultural translation. He was likely one of the first individuals to translate Japanese literature into Ukrainian, introducing readers to classical Japanese thought through works such as *Hōjōki* by Kamo no Chōmei and *Kōjinbutsu no fūfu* (*An Amiable Couple*) by Shiga Naoya[36]. His translations offered Ukrainian audiences a rare window into Japanese literary tradition and

---

36 *Hōjōki* (*An Account of My Hut*) is a 1212 essay by Kamo no Chōmei reflecting on impermanence and reclusion. *Kōjinbutsu no fūfu* (*An Amiable Couple*) is a 1910 short story by Shiga Naoya, often regarded as the 'god of the novel' in modern Japanese literature.

exemplified his commitment to fostering cross-cultural understanding.

He also authored two collections of essays reflecting on his life in both Paris and Lviv. His writing style is captivating—elegant yet intimate. In his vivid recollections of Paris, he evokes the aroma of coffee and freshly baked bread in corner cafés, the soft fragrance of flowers in the Luxembourg Garden, and the quiet stillness of the Louvre's galleries on early Sunday mornings. These evocative details draw the reader in, stirring a desire to walk the same streets and see the world through Levynskyi's reflective, cosmopolitan eyes.

His essays on life in Paris and Lviv were widely read and admired for their insight, vivid detail, and engaging personal tone. In Paris, Stepan Levynskyi refined his ability to see the global in the personal, skillfully connecting Ukrainian subjectivity with broader transnational currents. At the same time, Lviv played a central role in shaping his worldview. The city's Catholic rigidity and Central European traditions provided him with a strong foundation in discipline, culture, and education, but they also instilled in him a quiet yearning for something more expansive, freer, and less confined. His reflections often carry an implicit contrast between the vibrant, multicultural life he discovered abroad—particularly in places like Paris and the more restrained, provincial yet aspiring central city atmosphere of home. And yet, Levynskyi never fully severed ties with Lviv. It remained the place that had given him his language, his sense of perspective, and the initial desire to build bridges between East and West. His writing consistently reveals this dual pull of rootedness and restlessness, of belonging and departure.

From his time living in Paris, Stepan Levynskyi maintained a strong awareness of his Ukrainian identity, which clearly permeates his writings. Even in conversations with Japanese and French acquaintances, he firmly insisted that he was Ukrainian—not Russian. This assertion of national identity is particularly significant given that Levynskyi was originally from Western Ukraine, a region that only became part of the Soviet Union in 1939—by which point he was already living in Asia. At the time, Japanese understanding of Ukraine was limited, and much of it came through personal encounters. In *Letters from the Japanese House*, Levynskyi's character Akira expresses an impression of Ukrainians shaped largely by Levynskyi himself, describing them as people "cast aside in life by the pressure of violent waves"—a poetic reflection of a displaced, misunderstood nation seen through the lens of one determined expatriate.

Living and working in Asia, Stepan Levynskyi not only supported the intellectual, social, and cultural life of the Ukrainian diaspora through his financial contributions and personal efforts but also remained deeply committed to the unification and independence of Ukraine. Newly uncovered documents from Polish archives suggest that Levynskyi was dispatched to Harbin by the Polish government to build connections with Ukrainians in the region and encourage support for *Prometheism*—a Polish geopolitical strategy aimed at weakening the Soviet Union by fostering nationalist movements among its non-Russian peoples, including Ukrainians, Georgians, and others. At the same time, documents from U.S. archives describe Levynskyi as a covert representative of the Ukrainian national movement in Asia, indicating that his role was not limited to Polish interests but was also part of a broader effort to promote Ukrainian self-determination.

When the short-lived state of Carpathian Ukraine was occupied by Hungary in March 1939—with Hungarian forces aligned with Nazi Germany—Levynskyi was so disturbed that he attempted to resign from his diplomatic position in Manchuria in protest. However, Ukrainian colleagues persuaded him to stay. A year later, he did leave his post and moved to Beijing, where he spent a year studying Chinese.

He then relocated to Shanghai, then under the influence of Chiang Kai-shek, where an estimated 5,000 Ukrainians lived. Levynskyi remained there for three months, assisting Ivan Svit with his publishing work. Unable to return to a Europe engulfed in war, he accepted a position in Saigon, in then French-controlled Vietnam, where from 1942 to 1946 he worked as an interpreter for the Governor of French Indochina.

Before going to study abroad, Stepan Levynskyi was briefly married in Lviv and had his only son named Yurii. His son became known as Jorge Lewinski (1921 – 2008) in Britain and rose to international recognition as a prominent British photographer who, from the 1960s onward, created a rich collection of portraits of the major figures of British art, now considered a vital archive of 20th-century British visual culture. Unfortunately, the father and son never met again after Stepan left for China.

However, Stepan's weakened health and the hardships he endured during the war took a significant toll on his body. On July 25th, 1946, he returned to France due to illness, and just a few months later, on October 8th, he passed away in the southern French city of Gap, in the province of Hautes-Alpes.

Stepan Levynskyi was a cosmopolitan who lived in many countries, an internationalist who befriended people of diverse backgrounds, and a dreamer of a world built on equality. As a writer, he had a keen eye and a brilliant ear for language, carefully selecting his words and often rewriting his work multiple times in pursuit of perfection. This dedication meant that he left behind only a small body of work – some might say his talent never fully blossomed, as he passed away just shy of 50. Yet what he did leave is exceptional. Ukrainian writer and head of Piramida Publishing House, Vasyl Gabor, who released two volumes of Levyskyi's writings in 2020, called his stories "a medicine for the Ukrainian intellectual's mind." His legacy is not only literary but cultural, offering a rare and thoughtful bridge between Ukraine and distant Japan.

Stepan Levyskyi was a remarkable figure whose life traced the arc of a restless, thoughtful cosmopolitan shaped by his Ukrainian identity but unbound by geography. From Lviv to Paris, Harbin to Saigon, he forged deep cultural bridges between East and West, and between individual experience and collective history. Whether writing about Japanese aesthetics, Ukrainian émigré life in Manchuria, or the quiet corners of Parisian cafés, Levyskyi brought to his work a rare combination of literary sensitivity, curiosity, and intellectual generosity.

His Ukrainian identity was shaped both by his roots and his deliberate cultural and political commitments. Born in 1897 in Lviv, which was part of the Austro-Hungarian Empire till 1918 and later interwar Poland till 1939, he was raised in a culturally vibrant, Ukrainian-speaking environment and belonged to a family deeply involved in national architecture and design. Though he lived much of his adult life abroad—in Antwerp, Paris, Harbin, Tokyo, Beijing, Shanghai, Vietnam, and elsewhere—he consistently identified as Ukrainian, not Polish or Russian, and used his writings, translations, and diplomatic work to promote Ukrainian culture. In Harbin, he supported the Ukrainian diaspora, financed the publication of the "Green Ukraine" map and the first Japanese-Ukrainian dictionary, and collaborated with Ivan Svit to amplify Ukraine's presence in Asia. His strong national consciousness, even while operating in multilingual, international settings, reflects a distinctly Ukrainian worldview shaped by the borderland experience and reinforced by empathy for other stateless and colonised peoples.

Though he left behind a modest number of texts—partly due to his perfectionism—what survives is extraordinary in tone and breadth. His writing defies narrow national frames, instead offering a vision of Ukrainian subjectivity as deeply informed by the global. At a time when both empire and nationalism were reshaping the world, Levynskyi imagined something different: a world in which cross-cultural understanding was not only possible, but essential.

In the end, his story is not only that of a Ukrainian in Asia or a European in Manchuria or Japan, but of a borderland mind searching for truth, dignity, and beauty across civilisations. His voice—witty, observant, humane—deserves to be heard again, not only as a historical curiosity but as a witness to a more connected, empathetic world.

Ukraine's Marco Polo
The Global Journey of Sofia Yablonska-Oudin (1907–1971)

In today's world, travelling around the globe is a common dream, especially among young people. Round-the-world plane tickets offered by some air companies allow travellers to visit up to 15 countries within a year—an adventure that has become increasingly accessible. But in the early 1930s, when commercial aviation was still in its infancy and it was highly unusual—even frowned upon—for women to travel alone: one Ukrainian woman defied expectations. Sofia Yablonska set off on a journey across continents by ship, car, carriage, boat, and even camel or horse. Armed with a camera and a notebook, she documented the world as she saw it—vividly, independently, and from a distinctly Ukrainian perspective.

Sofia and her husband Jean Oudin

Sofia Yablonska—who later adopted the French version of her name, Sophie, after moving to France—was born on May 15th, 1907, in the village of Tarasivka in what is now the Lviv region of Ukraine. She was the daughter of a Ukrainian Greek Catholic priest. At the time, Ukraine was divided by the Zbruch River: to the west lay Galicia, under the cultural and political influence of the Austro-Hungarian Empire and, later, Poland; to the east stretched territories dominated by the Russian Empire. For many in western Ukraine, crossing the Zbruch felt like entering a foreign country.

Sofia's father, Ivan, had once dreamed of becoming a doctor. But after falling in love with a priest's daughter—and in keeping with church customs—he gave up medicine and entered the priesthood in order to marry her. He believed that, if he could not heal bodies, he could at least heal souls through preaching. The couple had several children, but their marriage eventually fell apart, and they separated—a rare and painful event in a priestly family of that era.

Ivan, became intellectually drawn to the ideas of the Russian Orthodox Church and Russophile ideology, leading him to take his four children to southern Russia, where they lived for several years in the city of Taganrog. As a single father and priest, Ivan struggled to support his large family on his own. After seven years, disillusioned and facing hardship, he returned to his native western Ukraine. One of his sons, sadly, did not survive their time in Russia and died there. Ivan's return was not only prompted by practical concerns but also by a growing recognition of the gap between the ideological ideals that had once captivated him and the reality under Bolshevik rule. Disenchanted with both Russophile thinkers and the Soviet system, he reaffirmed his Ukrainian Greek Catholic faith. Eventually, he was assigned to a parish in the provincial town of Ternopil, roughly 100 kilometres from the Galician capital, Lviv.

Raised by such an openminded father, Sofia was exposed to Ukrainian, Austro-Hungarian, and Russian culture and language between the ages of 7 and 14. Curious and imaginative, she returned to Ukraine at the age of 14 where her brother ran a movie theatre in Ternopil, and Sofia became fascinated with the world of cinematography while helping him sell tickets at the box office. Seeing the screen light up with the landscapes of alluring and intriguing faraway cities in the dark cinema halls, she decided to pursue a career in cinematography. After a while she moved to Lviv, where she attended school, watched plays, and being realistic enough to learn some useful skills she took sewing classes. Seeing her brother trying to run a business, and apart from movies—her distant ideal world, she also wanted to acquire some hard skills and enrolled on a commercial course at the Lviv Trading and Commercial school. Sophia had experienced moving from place to place since she was a small child, and her father was an important role model and a person she would ask for advice. Also, after multiple trips over seven years and an unsettled childhood home life *then* experiencing World War I, she eventually became a drifter, a kind of free soul looking for the stimulation of new things, experiences and it seemed she was unable to settle down.

Conservative Lviv quickly proved too small and stifling for the curious, ambitious Sofia. Paris—then the capital of fashion, cinema, and vibrant intellectual life—offered exactly the kind of stimulation she craved. In 1927, at the age of 20, Sofia made the bold move to the French capital to pursue studies at a film school. Having helped her brother successfully run two cinemas back in Lviv, she was able to fund her journey—a remarkable achievement for a young woman from what was still a provincial city.

Paris in the late 1920s, however, was no easy place for someone without wealth or connections. Sofia faced financial hardships but met them with grit, determination, and a ready smile. To support herself, she took on a wide range of jobs: cleaning, sewing, interpreting, cabaret dancing, working as a fashion model,
and even appearing as a film extra. Despite these challenges, she never gave up on her dream of becoming a photographer or cinematographer.

From a young age, Sofia had always admired beauty—no matter how little she had, her aesthetic sense remained sharp. She was sporty, stylish, and strikingly attractive. Her personal style—an elegant blend of the traditional and the modern—turned heads on Parisian streets. Sofia's presence radiated both the poise of a Ukrainian heritage and the daring spirit of a modern European woman.

At the time, following the fall of the Ukrainian People's Republic (1917–1921) and the loss of short-lived Ukrainian independence, many prominent Ukrainians—including former politicians and high-ranking military officers—were living in exile in France. A sizable Ukrainian émigré community had taken root in Paris, and Sofia found herself drawn into its intellectual and cultural life. She became friends with Stepan Levynskyi, who was studying Japanese in the city. Through him, she heard vivid stories about Asia that sparked her fascination with the East and planted the seed of her desire to travel there. It was likely in Paris that Sofia first met people from Japan and China, encounters that expanded her worldview and deepened her interest in non-European cultures.

Bold and intellectually curious, Sofia also initiated correspondence with Volodymyr Vynnychenko (1880–1951) — the former head of the Ukrainian People's Republic, a writer, and playwright — who was then living in exile in Austria and later France. Sofia, aspiring to become a writer, hoped Vynnychenko would become a mentor. However, his diary reveals a dismissive attitude, noting her beauty more than her literary potential and doubting her talent. In the end, Sofia proved him wrong. Her later published works not only gained recognition but also established her as a serious writer and one of the earliest Ukrainian female travel authors.

Sofia carefully saved money and, beginning in 1931, started travelling and writing travelogues. In 1932, after her journey to North Africa, she published her first travel book, *The Charm of Morocco*, in Ukraine. The book, beautifully written and richly descriptive, offers a vivid portrait of Morocco — then a French colony — through the eyes of a perceptive outsider who looked not from above, but from below, with deep respect and fascination for the local culture. Her travelogue doesn't merely describe sights — it evokes smells, sounds, and sensations, demonstrating her sensitivity and ability to perceive the world with all her senses. "I returned from the square intoxicated by the smell of sweaty bodies, grilled mutton, oil and oranges, and the lively Arab dances and music of the Berbers," she wrote. For Sofia, photography and writing were inseparable — each enhancing the other. As she confessed in her book, Morocco offered "so much inspiration, surprise and excitement, and so much richness and heat of form and colour, that I would rather send it to you right away in a photograph in one shot than write it out one by one on paper." During her travels, even locals complimented her sharp powers of observation—rare for a foreign visitor, let alone a solo woman traveller at the time.

As Sofia travelled the world, as she states in her writings, she consistently introduced herself as Ukrainian, proudly stating that Ukraine was home to 40 million people. Even as a young woman in her 20s, she carried a strong sense of national identity. In today's terms, she was engaging in a form of public diplomacy—representing Ukraine abroad at a time when it no longer existed as an independent state. In her travel writings, she often reflected on Ukraine's future, drawing parallels between her homeland—absorbed into the USSR after its short-lived independence in the 1910s-early 1920s—and the colonised nations of Asia and Africa.

Though she was a white European woman, Sofia understood and sympathised with the struggles of colonised peoples. Her perspective was not shaped by the inherent feeling of superiority common to many Western travellers of her era. Rather, she approached the cultures she encountered with respect and admiration, documenting their daily lives, customs, and aspirations. Unlike colonial travel writers, Sofia did not impose judgment—she listened, observed, and recorded, seeing herself not as a conqueror but as a guest. Her journeys were a statement of solidarity with the oppressed, and her writing a quiet but powerful expression of anti-colonial awareness.

Sofia Yablonska's *The Charm of Morocco* evokes the spirit of *One Thousand and One Nights*—not as an outsider gazing at an exotic world, but as a keen observer immersed within it. Her portrayals of local cultures and customs are filled with genuine respect and curiosity.

During her first journey to Asia, particularly China, she sought traces of traditional life amidst the chaos and uncertainty of modernising streets. In her travelogue *From the Land of Rice and Opium* (1936), she writes vividly about the remnants of old China that still thrived in narrow alleyways:

"You can find old-fashioned China in the side alleys. In stores with open doors, Chinese people card cotton and make fabric, tailor traditional deep-coloured clothes, make tableware out of copper, rings out of gold and silver, knives and axes out of iron, and buckets and large coffins out of wood. The coffins were made so solid that not only the dead but also their souls could not escape. Next to that store was a dental clinic, where a hole was drilled in a healthy front tooth and a gold tooth gem is placed in it as a symbol of wealth. Chinese dentists who had studied abroad and returned home created this trend."

Her observations are rich not only in cultural detail but also in sensory and emotional texture, showing her deep engagement with the places she visited — not as a tourist, but as a thoughtful chronicler of a rapidly changing world.

While travelling in China, Sofia Yablonska began to distinguish social class through subtle markers, such as clothing, and she observed that people in the countryside seemed more open and genuine, greeting her with warm, honest smiles. For Sofia, immersing herself in a foreign land meant engaging with its colours, tastes, and sounds — and China, in all its intensity, felt profoundly alive. Her vivid travelogue captures the rhythms of daily life with cinematic clarity, pulling readers into the streets alongside her. She wrote:

"I am caught in the whirlwind of the hustle and bustle of the city, where Chinese people talk loudly, hop on their rides, run, and ring bells. The singing of the merchants and the chiming of the rickshaws' bells overtakes all the noise."

Sofia's writing invites readers not just to see, but to hear and feel the heartbeat of a world both foreign and fascinating.

Still, even as Sofia Yablonska immersed herself in the realities of China, her thoughts often returned to her homeland, Ukraine. In *From the Land of Rice and Opium*, she sharply observed that if Ukrainians possessed the same tenacity as Chinese farmers — who managed to harvest crops up to three times a year — then Ukraine, blessed with its rich black soil, could become the leading agricultural nation in Europe within a decade. While China was often dismissed by the West as backward in diplomacy, she saw it differently: the Chinese, she wrote, had a deep understanding of their land, produced fine crops, and cultivated a refined and enduring culture. At the same time, she did not idealise their situation — she recognised the crushing poverty many faced. Despite their cultural sophistication, many Chinese were struggling under the weight of material hardship. She also noted the irony that many so-called modern Western technologies had often complicated, rather than improved, daily life. One day, in a heartbreaking moment, she witnessed a mother selling her young son out of desperation — and unable to stand by, Sofia took the boy in as a foster parent.

The early 1930s preceded the rise of female filmmakers, and it was still extremely rare for a Western woman to travel solo through colonial territories with a camera in hand. For a young woman to journey the world alone was not only unconventional — it was often unsafe. Sofia, who frequently wore trousers, was sometimes mistaken for a boy while travelling through parts of Africa. However, in Asia, her tall and slender figure made her stand out, and it was impossible to blend in or go unnoticed.

Sophia documented her travels not only through writing but also with photography and 8 mm film. At the time, French film companies were eager to acquire local footage to present to potential investors and developers and expand their presence in the colonies, and Sophia was contracted as a special correspondent. However, photography was still a relatively new technology, and in parts of China, there were superstitions surrounding the camera — some believed it could steal a person's soul. As a result, Sophia often had to hide her equipment and work discreetly. In one instance, she rented a space in a building facing a busy street under the pretense of opening an "Import/Export Store." She hung a yellow screen over the window to obscure her camera and covered the glass with eye-catching flyers to draw passersby's attention. While people stopped to read the posters, she secretly photographed them. Once her project was complete, she quietly shut down the "store," announcing its "bankruptcy," and moved on before anyone realised her true purpose.

Starting in 1932, Sofia embarked on a nearly two-year journey around the world. From Paris, she travelled through Marseille, Port Said, Djibouti, Colombo, China, Saigon, Singapore, Java, Bali, Australia, New Zealand, Tahiti, San Francisco, and New York. Although she had hoped to visit Japan, she extended her stay in China instead. There, she met and fell in love with Jean Oudin, a French engineer who would later become a diplomat. They married in 1933 and settled in Kunming, in China's Yunnan province. During their time in Asia, the couple was blessed with three children. At one point, her husband also served as the French diplomatic representative to China.

Sofia's diaries documenting her life and travels across Asia were published throughout the 1930s in the Galician women's magazine *Nova Khata* ("New Home"). Following the publication of *The Charm of Morocco* in 1932 and *From the Land of Rice and Opium* in 1936, she released another travelogue titled *Distant Horizons* (*Daleki Obrii* in Ukrainian) around 1939, covering her journeys in French Polynesia, Australia, and New Zealand. Her writing reached Ukrainians as far away as China, who followed her travels through these publications and began corresponding with her. Sofia also contributed short stories to Ukrainian women's magazines; one such story featured a Japanese woman, likely someone Sofia had met during her time in Paris. The narrative tells the tragic tale of a 19-year-old woman named Yukiko who travelled to Paris aspiring to become a film actress. She fell in love with a French artist but, realising that the relationship stifled her creative spirit, eventually left him—only to end her life in despair.

Believing deeply in the power of the camera to capture a fleeting moment, Sofia Yablonska dedicated herself to documenting local cultures through film and photography. At a time when strict gender roles defined women's lives, her solo travels were a quiet act of rebellion — an assertion of independence and creative freedom. In her final work, dedicated to her father, she reflected that one of the most important lessons he taught her was "to leave your efforts to posterity." Sofia did just that. She preserved glimpses of foreign customs, faces, colours, and everyday beauty — transforming them into literature, photographs, gardens, and memories that have endured beyond her lifetime. Engaging with her work feels like stepping into a time machine, travelling alongside a sharp-eyed, curious woman who roamed the world with both wonder and purpose. Her vivid, sensory writing pulls the reader into her journeys as if walking beside her. Always seeking an ideal world of beauty and freedom, Sofia Yablonska was, in every sense, a pioneer — a female Marco Polo of the early 20th-century.

During Sofia's time in China, World War II broke out in Europe, and in 1939 the Red Army occupied Western Ukraine. The news deeply affected her father, contributing to his death. Sofia, who had been profoundly attached to him, was devastated by her inability to return home for the funeral — an absence that left a lasting emotional scar. As the war intensified, the Ouden family relocated from China to French Indochina due to her husband's diplomatic assignments. With the onset of decolonisation in Asia, they returned to Paris in 1946, bringing Sofia's mother with them from Soviet-occupied Western Ukraine. Sadly, just two years later, in 1948, her mother passed away in France.

Having witnessed so much beauty during her travels in the East, Sophia drew on that inspiration to launch a successful floral arrangement and interior design business in Paris. Yet her life was also marked by personal tragedy. She lost one of her sons in the Algerian War, and in 1955, her beloved husband Jean passed away. Honouring his dream, Sophia built a house on the island of Noirmoutier, along France's Atlantic coast, based on sketches they had made together. There, she spent her later years creating floral designs, shaping interiors, and writing. In 1977, she completed *A Book about My Father: From My Childhood*, a moving tribute to the man who had shaped her spirit. Though written in Paris, the book was only published in Ukraine in 2015, where it drew widespread attention and renewed interest in her legacy.

Sofia died in a tragic car accident on February 4th, 1971, at the age of 63, while on her way to deliver a new manuscript to the publishing house. The book, titled *Two Weights, Two Measures*, was published posthumously the following year, serving as a final testament to her sharp observations and unwavering literary voice.

When Sophia decided to travel around the world, she imagined discovering a distant, untouched paradise—some place beyond the turmoil of history and politics. But as she later reflected in *Distant Horizons*, "Even though I travelled to many places, I have never found the heaven I imagined. Yet sometimes, I saw an ordinary happy shine, that was more valuable to me than any heaven I could have imagined. So I walk the long road that is stretching in front of me. Despite many hardships and difficulties that await me. Along the way, I would enjoy the precious beauty of the East." These words capture the essence of her journey—not a quest for escape, but a deeper engagement with life's fleeting moments of joy and wonder.

All the precious moments from her travels and her life in China, Sofia Yablonska transformed into photographs and evocative stories. Her work became more than a personal archive — it became a wellspring of courage for others. Courage to search for a place where one truly belongs. Courage to create, to question, to speak out. Courage to live authentically, despite convention. Through her lens and her words, Sofia offered a vision of freedom — freedom to dream, to explore, and to remain true to oneself in a world that often discourages such boldness.

Sofia's Ukrainian identity was shaped by both origin and choice. Born in 1907 in what then Austrian-ruled Galicia and later part of Poland was, she came from a Ukrainian Greek Catholic priestly family and was immersed in a culturally Ukrainian environment from childhood. Though she spent a few years in the Russian Empire with her father, she returned to western Ukraine as a teenager, where her love for cinema and language blossomed. Later, living in Paris and travelling across the globe, she consistently identified herself as Ukrainian — despite Ukraine's political nonexistence at the time — and presented its culture with pride. Through her writings, she often drew parallels between colonised nations and her homeland, expressing solidarity with oppressed peoples and framing Ukraine's struggle for identity as part of a broader global condition. Her work, life, and voice remained deeply rooted in Ukrainian experience, even as she moved across continents.

Sofia Yablonska-Oudin was a visionary traveller, writer, and documentarian whose life defied the expectations of her time. In an era when few women ventured far from home — let alone across continents — Sofia crossed borders with a camera in hand and a deep curiosity in her heart. She explored the world not as a colonial observer, but as a respectful guest, engaging with cultures on equal terms and capturing their beauty through photography and prose. Her Ukrainian roots remained central to her identity, and she often used her unique perspective to draw parallels between the struggles of colonised peoples and her homeland's quest for freedom.

Through her vivid storytelling and images, she invited readers into worlds unfamiliar and far-flung, offering glimpses of everyday life, spiritual richness, and cultural dignity. But perhaps most importantly, she became a model of courage—of how to remain open, self-aware, and creative in the face of hardship. Her legacy is not only one of adventure and artistic talent, but of deeply lived human experience—one that continues to inspire those who seek to understand others and themselves. Like a true female Marco Polo of the 20th-century, Sofia Yablonska charted new paths—for women, for Ukrainians, and for global citizens alike.

A Prince by Birth, a Ukrainian by Choice
Vasyl Vyshyvanyi
Archduke Wilhelm Franz von Habsburg-Lothringen
(10.02.1895-18.08.1948)

In the sweltering August of 1948, a 53-year-old Ukrainian military officer, emaciated from prolonged torture in Kyiv's Lukyanivska Prison, was buried in an unmarked grave. His death, the result of abuse and neglect, was tragically common in Soviet prisons of the time, where countless political prisoners perished without funeral rites. But this man's background was anything but ordinary. His name was Wilhelm Franz of Austria—more widely known as Wilhelm von Habsburg-Lothringen—the youngest son of the illustrious Habsburg-Lothringen dynasty. A recently declassified report from April 1948, written by Soviet secret police chief Viktor Abakumov to Nikita Khrushchev, then First Secretary of the Communist Party of Ukraine, refers to "Wilhelm Habsburg-Lothringen, a British and French spy." The letter is now part of the archival records of the Security Service of Ukraine (SBU).

After World War II, Vienna was divided into zones of occupation by the Allied powers, and Soviet troops controlled part of the city. In August 1947, Wilhelm von Habsburg left his residence at Fasangasse 49, near Vienna's Belvedere Palace—and never returned. He was arrested by the Soviet secret police (KGB) and transported to the Ukrainian capital, Kyiv.

Wilhelm was born on February 10th, 1895, in the Adriatic port city of Pula (in present-day Croatia), surrounded by pine forests and fig groves along the coast. Like most men in his aristocratic family, he graduated from a military academy and began a career in uniform. He was a member of the Habsburg-Lothringen dynasty—one of Europe's most powerful royal houses—and later joined the Austrian People's Party in the turbulent years following the fall of the empire.

Wilhelm's father, Archduke Karl Stephan of Austria, was the son of the younger brother of Emperor Franz Joseph I, who ruled the Austro-Hungarian Empire for an extraordinary 68 years. Karl Stephan married the daughter of a Tuscan archduke, and together they had six children. A devoted admirer of Polish culture, Karl Stephan owned estates in Galicia and maintained several castles there. He ensured that his children were educated in the Polish language and traditions. Two of his daughters married into Polish noble families, and Wilhelm's elder brother, Karl Albrecht, followed their father's path, fully embracing a Polish identity and becoming active in Polish political and military life.

As a young man, Wilhelm travelled extensively with his father on ethnographic expeditions, visiting places such as North Africa and Constantinople by ship. These journeys were not merely for leisure—they served as a kind of field education in geography, culture, and political science. For a time, the family went to Galicia (today's Western Ukraine), a region often called a microcosm of the Habsburg Empire due to its rich mix of ethnic groups: Ukrainians, Poles, Hutsuls, Romanians, Hungarians, Jews, and others. Immersed in this diverse environment, Wilhelm developed a deep appreciation for Ukraine and its people. He began studying the Ukrainian language and culture, gradually forming a strong emotional and intellectual attachment to the Ukrainian cause.

After graduating from military school in 1915, Wilhelm was assigned to a Ukrainian unit within the Austro-Hungarian army. Fluent in his mother's native Italian and his father's German, he also embraced Ukrainian as a personal choice—a language he not only learned but used to write poetry. His affection for Ukrainian culture was unmistakable. He took to wearing traditional Ukrainian embroidered shirts (vyshyvankas) beneath his military uniform, a gesture that earned him the nickname *Vasyl Vyshyvanyi*, or "Vasyl the Embroidered." His outward display of solidarity with the Ukrainian people went beyond symbolism — it marked the beginning of his political and cultural transformation.

When German and Austrian troops entered Ukraine in early 1918, it was ostensibly at the request of the Ukrainian Central Rada, which was seeking support in its struggle against the Bolsheviks. However, the broader geopolitical reality was more complex. After signing the Treaty of Brest-Litovsk with the Central Powers, the Bolsheviks effectively ceded Ukraine to German and Austrian control. The Central Powers were less motivated by a genuine interest in Ukrainian independence and more by their own strategic and economic goals — primarily securing access to grain, coal, and cheap labour. When the Central Rada proved unable to deliver on these demands, the Germans staged a coup and installed Hetman Pavlo Skoropads'kyi (1873-1945) as a more compliant leader. Skoropads'kyi ruled as Skoropads'kyi of the Ukrainian State from April to December 1918.

During this turbulent period, Wilhelm fought in Zaporizhzhia and Kherson, aligning himself with Ukrainian aspirations. While stationed in Zaporizhzhia, he instructed his men to study Cossack history and promoted the Ukrainianisation of his unit. His efforts inspired a sense of national identity among the Ukrainian peasants he conscripted. Rumours spread across the region that Wilhelm — already affectionately known as *Vasyl Vyshyvanyi* for his fondness for Ukrainian embroidered shirts — might even aspire to become a monarch of an independent Ukraine.

After the brief and ultimately unsuccessful period of Ukrainian independence, Wilhelm returned to Vienna — but he never abandoned the Ukrainian cause. In 1921, he became the head of the Ukrainian National Free Cossack Society in Vienna and, under the pen name *Vasyl Vyshyvanyi*, published a collection of poems in Ukrainian titled *The Days Pass*, dedicated "To

Those Who Died for Ukraine's Freedom." In it, he called on the Ukrainian Sich Riflemen, whom he had once led, to continue the struggle for Ukraine's independence.

During World War II, Vyshyvanyi remained in Austria and refused to collaborate with the Nazis. Evidence suggests that he maintained covert contacts between Ukrainian nationalist circles and the French government and engaged with British intelligence. He was in close communication with Yevhen Konovalets (1891-1938), the leader of the Organisation of Ukrainian Nationalists (OUN), and later with Andriy Melnyk (1890-1964), who succeeded Konovalets after his assassination.

You may wonder why *Vasyl Vyshyvanyi* (Wilhelm Habsburg) was considered such a dangerous figure by Soviet authorities even after World War II had ended. The answer lies in the Soviet regime's deep fear of nationalism. The USSR was a federation of republics with distinct cultures, languages, and religions—held together largely by the dominance of the Russian language and Soviet ideology. If any of these republics, particularly Ukraine—the second most significant Soviet republic—began asserting its own ethnic identity and national ambitions, the unity of the Soviet state could be seriously threatened.

Ukraine had briefly enjoyed independence between 1918-1919, and although that period ended with Soviet annexation, many of its political and cultural leaders fled into exile in cities such as Prague, Paris, Berlin, and London. There, they established a robust network to support the cause of Ukrainian independence from abroad: founding libraries and even a Ukrainian university in exile, publishing newspapers and journals, and holding political rallies to maintain national consciousness.

The Soviet authorities monitored these activities closely and undertook systematic efforts to eliminate their leadership. Among the most notable assassinations were the following three people. Symon Petliura (1879-1926), a key leader of the Ukrainian People's Republic and commander of its army, who was assassinated in Paris in May 1926; Yevhen Konovalets (1891-1938), head of the Organisation of Ukrainian Nationalists (OUN) and a former colonel in the Ukrainian army, who was killed by a bomb disguised as a gift in Rotterdam in May 1938—an operation orchestrated by the NKVD; Stepan Bandera (1909-1959), the ideological leader of the OUN, assassinated in Munich in 1959 by a Soviet agent using a poison-laced umbrella.

All three were seen as potent symbols of Ukrainian resistance, and their elimination was part of the Soviet effort to crush national movements. Wilhelm Habsburg, who had ties with at least one of these figures, was viewed in a similar light: a charismatic, well-connected figure with royal lineage and nationalist sympathies—qualities that made him too dangerous to be left alone.

The fact that Wilhelm spoke fluent Ukrainian only worsened his case in the eyes of the Soviet authorities, as it was seen as further proof of his nationalist convictions. After being imprisoned in Kyiv, he was taken almost daily to the KGB headquarters on Volodymyrska Street 33—a building that still stands to-

Colonel K. Guzhkobskyi and Prince Wilhelm, around 1918

day—for interrogation. Despite being questioned in Russian, Wilhelm insisted on replying in Ukrainian, underscoring his identification with the Ukrainian cause. His responses were recorded by others in Russian, further distancing his voice from the official narrative. To his interrogators, he must have appeared not only as a political enemy, but as a deeply confusing one—a foreign-born aristocrat who spoke Ukrainian like a native and embodied the very idea of a free, multiethnic Ukraine.

Scholars of Ukrainian history regard Archduke Wilhelm of Habsburg, also known as *Vasyl Vyshyvanyi*, as a complex figure: an intellectual, a poet, and a committed advocate for Ukrainian independence. According to American historian Timothy Snyder, Wilhelm's embrace of Ukraine was not only political but deeply personal—a defiance of his aristocratic lineage and a search for identity and belonging. Snyder suggests that Wilhelm's affinity for Ukraine, a nation historically caught between the Habsburg and Russian empires, stemmed from his identification with the plight of statelessness. To illustrate Wilhelm's multifaceted life, Snyder colour-codes its phases: blue for childhood, red for his years in the military, white for his imperial heritage, and orange for his resistance to both Stalinism and Nazism. Snyder also notes Wilhelm's artistic flair, interest in fashion and music, a small tattoo hidden beneath his wristwatch, and his homosexuality, suggesting a personality marked by both charisma and contradiction—a free spirit who, despite personal complexities, remained devoted to the Ukrainian cause.

At the end of the interrogations, Vasyl Vyshyvanyi was sentenced to 25 years in a Kyiv prison on charges of espionage. However, he was so physically weakened by torture and deprivation that he did not survive to serve his sentence—he died shortly after. Ironically, just three years after Viktor Abakumov (1908–1954) had written a letter to Nikita Khrushchev accusing Wilhelm of spying for the Germans and British, the former head of the Soviet secret police was himself arrested during Stalin's purges. In 1951, Abakumov was executed, accused of being a Zionist spy—a grim reflection of the very paranoia and repression he once directed at others.

Conclusion
Borders and Beyond: The Ukrainian Spirit

Unlike Japan or Great Britain, Ukraine is a rolling terrain not bounded by the natural barrier of the sea, making defence an urgent priority for whoever ruled it. In ancient times, nomadic peoples roamed the lands of present-day Ukraine, and by the 12th-century, the Kyivan Rus' — a loose federation of principalities centered in Kyiv — faced frequent internal conflict, including attacks from rival neighbouring principalities. Despite occasional efforts at unity, these polities often failed to consolidate against external threats from the steppe. The region's geography, including the Dnipro and Dniester rivers, positioned it as a vital corridor for trade between the Baltic and Black Seas, as well as a gateway linking Central Europe to the broader Eurasian world.

In the Middle Ages, the territories of present-day Ukraine experienced successive waves of control by various powers, most notably the Tatars (Kipchaks) — successors to the Mongol Empire — who dominated the steppe and exerted influence over the region long after the Mongol Empire itself had fragmented. Over time, these lands also came under the rule or incursion of the Ottomans, Poles, Austrians, Russians, Swedes, and Germans. As historian Kelly O'Neill has observed, for much of Ukraine's recorded history, it was the world of the steppe — mobile, decentralised, and often imperial — that held sway over the more settled agricultural plains[37].

However, there were Cossacks — especially Ukrainian Cossacks from the 15th-century onward — who moved to the edges of empires, settling in the steppes where there were no fixed borders and where state authority held little sway. Many of them fled serfdom and slavery in Polish-Lithuanian or Muscovite lands, seeking freedom in these frontier zones. There, they lived autonomously and practiced defence arms freely, forming self-

---

37 For more see O'Neill, Kelly. *Claiming Crimea: A History of Catherine the Great's Southern Empire*. New Haven: Yale University Press, 2017.

governing military communities. They earned their livelihood by organising into armies and often hiring themselves out as mercenaries. This tradition of semi-nomadic military life distinguished them from the later Russian Cossacks, who, from the 17th-century, were more formally incorporated into the Tsarist military apparatus and used as agents of imperial expansion and border control.

There is a well-known Ukrainian saying: *"My house is on the edge"* (*моя хата скраю*). At first glance, this might seem to express indifference or passivity, but in reality, it often reflects a deeper desire for autonomy and self-preservation. It implies that one prefers to live freely, without interference — a mindset shaped by centuries of surviving as individuals or families amid instability, rather than relying on collective structures. Interestingly, the phrase echoes a broader cultural and linguistic ambiguity. The word *"kray"* (край) in Ukrainian means both "edge" and "land," and some scholars have linked this to the debated etymology of *"Ukraina."* Some interpret *"Ukraina"* as meaning "borderland" — a place on the edge — while others argue it derives from an older Slavic usage meaning "homeland." This dual meaning — being both at the margins and at home — captures the historical tension Ukrainians have navigated: living at the crossroads of empires while continuously seeking a stable sense of identity and belonging.

For Ukrainians, perceptions of borders have historically differed between east and west — not in clarity, but in character. The eastern frontier, opening onto the vast steppe and toward Muscovy, was more fluid and expansive, with Cossack campaigns reaching into Ottoman and Tatar territories. Yet the western borderlands — regions like Halychyna, Bukovina, and Volyn — were also deeply contested and ethnically diverse, especially in the 19th and 20th centuries. While the Zbruch and Buh rivers were seen by many Poles as natural eastern boundaries of their state, Ukrainians envisioned their historical homeland stretching deep into the Carpathian foothills, sometimes even to Kraków and Rzeszów.

Even in the 17th-century, Cossack leaders understood the importance of the west. Bohdan Khmelnytsky led his forces into

Halychyna during the uprising against the Polish-Lithuanian Commonwealth, and Ivan Vyhovsky, in the draft of the Union of Hadiach, positioned himself as a defender of all Orthodox Christians within Polish lands. Although the Cossack imagination was often drawn south and eastward, toward confrontation and freedom on the steppe, their ambitions—and the cultural geography of Ukraine—always spanned in multiple directions.

The legacy of the Cossacks remains vivid in Turkish memory, where two kinds of folk songs still circulate: in some, the Cossacks are portrayed as bold and brotherly allies; in others, they are seen as fierce invaders and ruthless enemies. This dual image reflects the complex role Cossacks played in the region's history. After the destruction of the Zaporizhzhian Sich in 1775 and the subsequent absorption of the Cossack Host into the centralised Russian Empire, many Cossacks dispersed. Seeking to preserve their traditions of autonomy and free life, some migrated to the Kuban and Don regions or even as far as the Amur River in the Russian Far East, settling in areas where imperial control was looser and borders were more porous.

However, not all resisted incorporation. A portion of the Cossack *starshyna* (elite officers) chose to integrate into the Russian *dvorianstvo* (nobility) and served the Tsarist state, especially in its borderland expansions. Thus, the Cossack legacy splits between those who continued to seek freedom at the empire's periphery and those who found new roles within its structures of power.

In the 18th and early 19th centuries, the borders of the Russian Empire were extended deep into the Far East and across the Pacific, often with the involvement of Ukrainians—particularly those descended from Cossack lineages. Among them was Yurii Lysianskyi (1773—1837), an imperial navy officer who, in 1803, co-led the first Russian circumnavigation of the globe aboard the Neva. A cosmopolitan figure, he had studied with the British Royal Navy and lived in the United States before joining the Russian expedition. Today he is often remembered as a Russian explorer, but Lysianskyi was, in fact, a Ukrainian from a prominent Cossack family in Nizhyn, in the Chernihiv region. His legacy is marked across the globe, with a mountain and a river on Sakhalin and islands in Hawaii and Alaska bearing his name.

Yet to label him exclusively Ukrainian or Russian risks anachronism. In Lysianskyi's time, especially within the imperial elite, loyalty to the Romanov dynasty and service to the empire often took precedence over ethnic or national identity. As such, figures like Lysianskyi inhabited overlapping identities: Ukrainian by origin, Russian by imperial affiliation. His life reflects the broader entanglement of Ukrainian contributions within the machinery of Russian expansion—and the complex interplay between local identity and imperial purpose.

Ukrainian lands have long been under pressure, enslaved by other nations, and at the mercy of borders created by others.

The term "Ukrainian lands" can be understood in multiple ways and must be clearly defined. One interpretation refers to territories where ethnic Ukrainians and the Ukrainian language historically dominated. Another definition includes all regions that were at any time governed by a Ukrainian state. These distinctions produce different boundaries: the first might exclude Crimea while including parts of present-day Belgorod and Kursk oblasts in Russia, which had significant Ukrainian-speaking populations prior to the 1930s. The second definition would more likely include Crimea, based on its administrative status under Ukrainian governance, but exclude Belgorod and Kursk—aside from any territories currently under Ukrainian control.

Historically, naming rights and administrative norms were often imposed in foreign tongues—Polish, Russian, German—yet the reality was complex. Many Ruthenian (Orthodox) nobles assimilated into Polish or Russian elites for social mobility, while the Ukrainian-speaking peasantry remained rooted in local traditions. Assimilation often reflected class dynamics as much as identity.

Likewise, the idea that it was "easier" to live in borderless or loosely defined regions is questionable, as many saw borders as a threat. In the 18th and early 19th centuries, Ukrainian-speaking peasants rarely migrated far; serfdom, poverty, and political controls kept most tied to their villages. The mid-century abolition of serfdom in the Austrian (1848) and Russian (1861) empires loosened these bonds, but mobility was still limited by economic hardship and administrative restrictions. Seasonal labour, settlement in southern frontier lands, and, by the late 19th-century, migration to industrial centres, Siberia, or overseas became more common—yet for most, such movement was temporary, and the village remained their anchor.

By contrast, in centralised states like Britain or France, people may have lived with firmer borders but had access to broader institutional protections and opportunities for movement, including through imperial expansion. Ukrainian regions such as Halychyna were densely populated, under-resourced, and offered few such avenues of personal or geographical escape.

Japan, where I received my education, and Ukraine differ dramatically in their natural borders. In western Ukraine, the Carpathian Mountains form a natural barrier, and there is a longstanding perception that the lands beyond them are somehow "foreign." In fact, the Ukrainian name for the region beyond the Carpathians is *Zakarpattia*, which literally means "beyond the Carpathians"—known in English as Transcarpathia. Rivers, however, function differently. Unlike mountains, which tend to divide, rivers can both separate and connect: they may serve as borders where mountains are absent, or they may act as arteries of economic and cultural exchange. Cossacks once navigated down these rivers in their chaika boats[38], heading to the Black Sea.

Just as rivers in Japan can mark municipal boundaries, in Europe they often demarcate national ones. The Zbruch River, a tributary of the Dniester, is a poignant example. From 1772 to 1793 it marked the border between Poland and Austria; then, between the Austrian and Russian empires from 1793 to 1809 and again from 1815 to 1918; and later, from 1921 to 1939, it served as the

---

38 Chaika (*чайка* in Ukrainian meaning "seagull") was a type of light, manoeuverable wooden boat used by the Cossacks from the 16th to 18th centuries, especially by the Zaporizhian Cossacks for navigation along the Dnipro River and into the Black Sea. These vessels were typically about 20–25 metres long, powered by both oars and a sail, and were designed to carry up to 60–70 men. Chaikas were famously used in Cossack raids against Ottoman coastal strongholds and were central to the Cossacks' naval warfare and trade expeditions.

border between the USSR and the Republic of Poland. Today, it separates Ternopil and Khmelnytskyi oblasts within Ukraine. If the Zbruch could speak, it might tell countless stories—of war, exile, and shifting empires—and perhaps even move us to tears.

The Dnipro River, the longest in Ukraine, flows through Russia, Belarus, and Ukraine, connecting over 25 towns and cities along its path. More prominently, it has come to symbolise a rough divide within Ukraine itself—historically bisecting the country into a more European-oriented west and a Russian-influenced east. From 1667 to 1772, the Dnipro served as the southeastern frontier of the Polish-Lithuanian Commonwealth, anchoring its legacy as both a unifying artery and a cultural fault line.

Incidentally, the Dnipro River—known in Russian as the Dnepr—was referred to as *Borisfen* by the 5th-century BCE Greek historian Herodotus, a name likely of Scythian origin. This ancient name even appeared on 17th-century Dutch maps, reflecting its longstanding place in European geography. During the era of the Kyivan Principality, however, the river was called *Slavutych*, a name rooted in Old East Slavic. In the 20th-century, this historical resonance was revived when a new town built for the workers and families displaced by the Chornobyl nuclear disaster was named Slavutych, in honour of the river. This layering of names reflects Ukraine's deep and enduring connection to the Dnipro—etched in memory, geography, and national identity.

Among the three countries through which the Dnipro flows—Russia, Belarus, and Ukraine—it is in Ukraine that the river holds its greatest historical, cultural, and symbolic weight. Although the Dnipro originates in Russia and passes through southeastern Belarus, its longest and most demographically vital stretch lies within Ukraine, where it traverses over 1,000 kilometres and runs through major cities such as Kyiv, Dnipro, Zaporizhzhia, and Kherson. Historically, the Dnipro was central to the Kyivan Rus', serving as a vital artery in the Varangian–Greek trade route and later becoming the heartland of Cossack life, with the Zaporizhzhian Sich established along its lower reaches. The river is profoundly embedded in Ukrainian culture and national identity, appearing frequently in folklore and in the poetry of Taras Shevchenko as a symbol of both suffering and resilience.

In his poetry, Shevchenko depicts the Dnipro as a grand, masculine presence—both powerful and compassionate, a true father figure to the Ukrainian people. More than just a river, it emerges as a living force, deeply spiritual and steeped in historical memory. Shevchenko uses evocative epithets such as "roaring," "groaning," "mighty," "wide," "old," "grey," "holy," "steep-banked," "true father," and even calls it an "old Cossack." These images imbue the Dnipro with both the raw energy of nature and the proud, rebellious spirit of the Cossacks—central symbols in Ukrainian cultural identity. Unlike Russia, whose cultural identity is more closely tied to the Volga and Don, Ukraine regards the Dnipro not just as a river and not merely part of the landscape, but as a national hero, a witness to sorrow and resistance, and a reflection of Ukraine's enduring strength and character.

Today, as war once again defines its banks, the Dnipro serves as both a physical and symbolic frontier—Ukraine's national river in every sense.

Kyiv developed along both banks of the Dnipro River, commonly referred to as the right and left banks. However, this terminology can feel counterintuitive: when looking at a north-oriented map, the so-called right bank lies on the left side of the page, and the left bank on the right. This is because riverbanks are named from the perspective of looking downstream, not according to cardinal directions. While this convention is logical in geographic terms, it can feel disorienting—especially to those accustomed to fixed spatial references like north, south, east, and west.

In Ukraine, cardinal directions have historically played a less central role in everyday spatial awareness than in some other cultures, such as Japan. Most Ukrainians do not instinctively orient themselves northward unless aided by technology, a trait they share with many people around the world—including Americans. Although schoolchildren learn that moss grows on the north side of trees, such natural cues are of little use in urban environments.

That said, with the Russian invasion and the resulting need for real-time navigation, map literacy and directional awareness have sharply increased in recent years.

Historically, most people—whether in Ukraine, UK or Japan, or elsewhere—did not navigate using abstract coordinates like north or south. Before the widespread availability of printed maps or smartphones, orientation was rooted in lived experience: the direction of the river's flow, the rise of a hill, the position of the sun, or the sound of a nearby church bell. Only specialised professions—navigators, soldiers, architects, and cartographers—needed to think in terms of spatial grids or cardinal directions. For everyday people, place was relational, not geometric. In Ukraine, this tradition lingered well into modern times, especially in rural or organic urban environments. Even today, someone asking for directions might hear, "Turn left at the yellow kiosk and go past the white building next to the oak tree," rather than "Go east for 300 metres." This isn't about being "less precise"—it reflects a worldview in which geography is shaped by community memory and sensory landmarks rather than rigid systems. The war, with its reliance on digital maps and military grids, has challenged this intuitive, place-based logic and introduced a new, militarised geography into daily life. Digital navigation turned into a tool not just for convenience, but for survival.

Unlike in Japan, where printed maps are part of daily life and widely used by people of all ages, the relationship with maps in Ukraine has a more delicate and politicised history. During the Soviet era, geography education focused on the vast territory of the USSR, including Ukraine, but students rarely studied or created maps of their own towns or neighbourhoods. Mapping one's immediate surroundings wasn't encouraged, partly because maps were considered sensitive information. This mindset was a legacy of the Cold War, when maps were seen as tools of the military and intelligence services. In schools, high school students took pre-conscription training classes: boys were taught to read topographic military maps and handle weapons like Kalashnikov rifles, while girls were trained in basic first aid and wartime nursing. These military-preparatory courses were standard across all Soviet schools—

and even continued in universities until the late 1980s. The presence of bomb shelters and regular air raid drills reinforced the atmosphere of militarised preparedness. While orienteering was popular among outdoor sports enthusiasts and offered a path to genuine map literacy, for most Soviet citizens, maps remained associated with secrecy, defense, and authority—not with everyday navigation.

I myself only learned to read maps properly after moving to Japan. Unlike in Europe, where streets are typically named and clearly marked, Tokyo's layout can seem confusing to newcomers—street names are rare, and addresses follow a hierarchical number system. But once you grasp it, it's surprisingly logical. An address like "Tokyo, Shibuya 2-2-3-33" breaks down as: ward (Shibuya), district (2), block (2), building (3), and apartment (33).

In contrast, cities like Kyiv rely on street names, often honouring prominent individuals. This can lead to confusion—especially since multiple streets might share the same surname. For example, in Kyiv till decade ago there were two separate Kotsyubynskyy Streets: one named after Mykhailo Kotsyubynskyi, a celebrated Ukrainian writer of the19th-century, and the other after his son Yurii Kotsyubynskyy, a Soviet Bolshevik leader. Since locals usually omit first names when giving directions, it's easy to end up on the wrong street unless you know the difference. However, after 2015, Yurii Kotsyubynskyi Street was renamed as part of Ukraine's decommunisation process, which aimed to remove Soviet-era symbols and names from public spaces—making navigation in the city more straightforward.

Until recently, one of the main railway systems in Ukraine was called the South-Western Railway (*Pivdenno-Zakhidna Zaliznytsia*)—a name inherited from the Russian Empire, where it made sense geographically because Kyiv was located southwest of the imperial capital, St. Petersburg. However, from the point of view of modern Ukraine, the name was increasingly misleading, since the railway lines radiated in all directions—west, east, north, and south—from Kyiv. Despite more than 30 years of independence, the name had lingered as a relic of imperial-era cartography.

Fortunately, this has changed: Ukraine has consolidated its rail network under the unified and nationally meaningful name Ukrainska Zaliznytsia (Ukrainian Railways) — a move that reflects not only administrative coherence but also symbolic independence from the imperial past.

Sometime before COVID a Japanese friend of mine arrived in Kyiv by train for the first time. When they tried to follow signs to the "north exit," they were surprised to find that the so-called "north exit" was not actually located to the north. Instead, it led to what is locally known as the "old station entrance." Walking through the glass corridor above the platforms, they saw arrows pointing toward "east" and "west," but none towards the "north," which added to the confusion. This is not just a matter of station signage — it reflects a broader geographical disorientation that stems from Ukraine's historical position within empires. For a long time, Ukraine lacked geopolitical autonomy, and its spatial orientation was defined with reference to imperial centres like Moscow. Even in academic discourse before the war, Russia was sometimes called Ukraine's "northern partner" — despite the fact that Belarus, not Russia, lies directly to Ukraine's north. As a result, the internal logic of Ukrainian geography has often been shaped by external points of reference, blurring the country's own directional self-perception.

Borders can shape not only territory but also a person's sense of self — including their name and language. Over centuries of shifting rule, many people living in what is now Ukraine were referred to not in their own tongue, but in the languages of outsiders. It is only recently that Ukrainian toponyms have been more widely recognised in their Ukrainian forms internationally — Kyiv instead of *Kiev*, Kharkiv instead of *Kharkov*, and Dnipro instead of *Dnepr*. Still, describing this as a simple return to the "original" names risks oversimplifying a complex history. In the era of Kyivan Rus', Kyiv would have appeared in Old Church Slavonic or other early East Slavic forms. Later, under Polish-Lithuanian rule, names were written in Chancery Ruthenian — a literary predecessor of modern Ukrainian, Belarusian, and Rusyn. Under the Russian Empire and Soviet Union, official usage shifted toward Russian forms, while other groups — Poles, Jews, Germans — used still different names, like *Lwów*, *Lemberg*, or *Odessa*. In some cases, the names we use now are not revivals of premodern ones: for instance, Dnipro is a modern post-Soviet name, replacing *Dnipropetrovsk*, but not reverting to older forms like *Yekaterinoslav* or *Novyi Kodak*. In this light, the modern naming of Ukrainian places is not simply a matter of restoring the past—it is a statement of cultural and political identity in the present.

Certainly, Ukraine is now better known internationally, and global awareness has made it somewhat easier to shift from "Kiev" to the Ukrainian "Kyiv," even if the latter remains challenging to pronounce in some languages. Renaming places in line with Ukrainian-language usage is more than a linguistic update—it is also a symbolic break from the country's colonial past and an assertion of national self-definition. Yet not all citizens have welcomed these changes. In regions like Donbas, where many residents identify with Russian language and culture due to long histories of imperial and Soviet-era settlement, such renamings have been perceived by some as erasures of their own identity. While the Ukrainian state sees these reforms as part of decolonisation and cultural restoration, others—particularly in Russian-speaking areas—have experienced them as top-down impositions that rewrite local histories. This tension highlights the complexity of nation-building in a historically multiethnic and multilingual society like Ukraine.

People living near Ukraine's western border have historically had a slightly different outlook than those in the east. The western frontier—shared with Poland, Slovakia, Hungary, and Romania—has long represented a boundary beyond which different lifestyles and more open social norms were perceived to exist. As early as the late 19th-century, proximity to these borders made it easier for residents of Galicia, Bukovina, and Transcarpathia to seek seasonal work or emigrate abroad, not only to Warsaw and Vienna, but across the Atlantic to the United States and Canada. Emigration became an established tradition in these areas. By contrast, central Ukraine, around Kyiv and the Dnipro basin, saw less outward migration except during moments of major upheaval such as World War I, the Russian Revolution, or collectivisation. In fact, rather than emigrating, these central and eastern territories sometimes attracted internal migration, including from ethnic Russians—particularly to the Donbas, Crimea, and the Black Earth belt—as part of tsarist and Soviet resettlement policies. These patterns contributed to the different demographic and cultural compositions of Ukraine's regions, which still influence attitudes toward borders and identity today.

Although the first maps of Ukrainian lands date back to the 16th-century, well into the 19th-century most maps in circulation were created by outsiders—and reflected borders imposed by foreign powers. Ukraine's territorial outlines were rarely drawn by Ukrainians themselves. As a famous Mexican-American (or Chicano) saying puts it, "We didn't cross the border, the border crossed us"—a sentiment that resonates deeply with Ukraine's historical experience. Under such conditions, Ukrainians often responded to borders in two opposing ways: either by ignoring them or by finding ways to transcend them. Over centuries of rule by empires and regimes that dictated boundaries from above, Ukrainians developed a cultural instinct for adapting to constraint—turning limitations into avenues of personal or communal freedom. In this sense, mastering the art of manoeuvring around imposed borders became not just a survival strategy, but a defining national skill.

The old-fashioned Ukrainian nimbleness in crossing borders—or operating at their confluence—has deep roots, tracing back to the Cossack era, and remains remarkably relevant today. As literary scholar Mary Louise Pratt has described, a "contact zone" is a space where cultures meet, clash, and negotiate. In this sense, Ukraine's borderlands, long shaped by overlapping empires and shifting frontiers, became dynamic zones of exchange rather than just lines of division. Ukrainians have historically learned to navigate these spaces with flexibility and pragmatism—turning geopolitical constraint into cultural fluency. This inherited skill of moving between worlds, adapting to competing powers while preserving identity, continues to define Ukraine's role on the modern geopolitical stage.

CONCLUSION 157

The Ukrainian capacity for cross-cultural communication has historically shaped its people in distinct ways. This adaptability — born of living at the crossroads of empires — has fostered a comfort with linguistic plurality, intercultural dialogue, and mobility. While it's true that Ukrainians may not be as globally dispersed as, for example, Jewish or Roma communities, and their diaspora is smaller than those of Poles or Germans, the Ukrainian experience is unique in how it internalises cultural multiplicity within its own borders. Ukraine has long been home to overlapping identities, religions, and languages, which cultivated figures like Mykola Hohol/Nikolai Gogol or Leopold von Sacher-Masoch (1836–1895) — individuals who could navigate and express multiple cultural registers at once.

Unfortunately, history is repeating itself. With the outbreak of the current Russo-Ukrainian war, borders once again take on an ambivalent role: the eastern frontier brings danger and displacement, while the western border evokes a sense of escape or liberation. As in the aftermath of the Russian Revolution a century ago, Ukrainians today are being forced to migrate — not out of choice, but survival — striving to rebuild lives and preserve identity in new and uncertain places.

Throughout this book, Ukraine emerges not simply as a clearly bounded territory, but as a dynamic point of convergence — a node in a wider network of ideas, identities, and movements. All of the individuals featured here were born within the lands we today call Ukraine, yet their lives unfolded across multiple cultural and imperial geographies: Kyiv/Kiev and Odesa/Odessa, certainly, but also Paris, Vienna, St. Petersburg, and even the Pacific. Their ambitions, identities, and creative output were shaped less by stable national borders than by mobility, translation, and the tension between empire and locality. In that sense, "Ukraine" functions in this book not only as a place, but as a condition — a crucible where overlapping allegiances, border-crossings, and hybrid identities produce modern lives.

Modernity, as it appears in these stories, is not anchored solely in nationhood or state-building, but in the pursuit of freedom, communication, and recognition across cultural boundaries. For some, this meant seeking space within imperial structures; for others, it required transcending those structures altogether. The enduring power of these lives lies in how they navigated constraint—with creativity, pragmatism, and resilience. In tracing their paths, we are invited to rethink Ukraine not as a periphery to larger civilisations, but as a generative frontier where the pressures of empire, war, and migration shaped distinctive forms of belonging. Seen this way, Ukraine becomes a lens through which we can understand the global condition of modernity itself: fractured, mobile, and always negotiating the space between imposed borders and chosen connections.

Nine individuals featured in this book—except for Skovoroda—were born in the territory of Ukraine between the 18th and 20th centuries. Despite living through turbulent times and facing an uncertain future, they each achieved remarkable accomplishments in fields such as art, aeronautics, medicine, and diplomacy. They crossed and overcame borders—geographical, political, and cultural. This book includes Ukrainians, Russians, Jews, and Poles, but most were born within Ukraine's borders. Their character was shaped by the unique environment of Ukraine: a geopolitical crossroads and historical melting pot that was multinational, multiethnic, multilingual, and multiconfessional. It was this diversity, forged by centuries of complex history, that gave rise to their resilience, creativity, and global perspective.

The last figure in this book, Prince Wilhelm, was an outsider by birth—but he chose Ukraine both culturally and politically. In doing so, he ultimately shared in Ukraine's fate, becoming a victim of the Soviet regime. Yet despite their diverse origins and life paths, all the individuals profiled here share key traits: remarkable flexibility, openness to communication, and a deep tolerance for different religions, cultures, languages, and ways of thinking. These qualities, shaped by Ukraine's unique historical landscape, enabled them to transcend boundaries and contribute meaningfully to the world around them.

Ukrainians have long held ambivalent feelings toward borders—experiencing them as sources of both insecurity and, paradoxically, freedom. This sense of freedom is not rooted in the existence of borders themselves, but in the persistent need to cross, negotiate, and overcome them. While borders have never resolved the region's deep historical tensions, they have shaped the Ukrainian people in distinctive ways—cultivating adaptability, resilience, and a capacity for dialogue across cultures. These traits may resonate especially with readers from relatively homogenous societies like Japan. But in truth, Ukraine's experience reflects a much larger global story. The lives featured in this book unfold against the backdrop of a world transformed by empires, mass migration, and the rise of nation-states. From the 18th to the 21st-century, people across the globe—from Central Europe to the Americas—have grappled with displacement, hybrid identity, and contested sovereignty. Seen in this light, Ukraine's history is not isolated but deeply entwined with global modernity: a story of individuals navigating thickening borders and expanding state power, and in doing so, shaping the modern world from its often-overlooked margins.

In a time of war and ongoing geopolitical upheaval, as Ukraine continues to fight for its very existence, I hope readers will find in the lives of these historical figures a quiet source of courage. Their paths—shaped by shifting empires, forced migrations, and uncertain borders—show how resilience, creativity, and human dignity can endure even in the harshest of circumstances.

While the concept of the Ukrainian nation is often tied to a shared language, territory, or historical narrative, this book suggests a more fluid and postmodern understanding. Rather than presenting a unified, fixed identity, Ukraine emerges here as a constellation of experiences shaped by movement, memory, and multiplicity. The ten individuals profiled in these pages lived across empires and ideologies, navigated shifting borders, and frequently bore multiple names and affiliations. Their "Ukrainianness" was not always inherited—it was often chosen, negotiated, or even rediscovered in exile.

In this sense, the Ukrainian nation can be understood as a postmodern project: layered, plural, and decentred. It exists not just within state borders but also in networks of diaspora, acts of cultural expression, and shared memory. Like postmodern identity itself, it resists simplification. This book explores Ukraine as a lived experience that defies rigid definitions—a place made real not only by geography, but by imagination, mobility, and connection.

More than anything, I hope this book brings Ukraine closer to the reader's heart and fosters a deeper understanding of a nation courageous enough to assert its right to exist, while continually navigating its identity and place in the world.

Historical Timeline

Year	Event
1648-1657	Khmel'nyts'kyi Uprising.
1654	Pereiaslav Union.
1667	The Truce of Andrusovo between Russia and Poland. Kyiv became a part of the Russian Empire though full control was solidified later in the 18th-century.
1700-1721	The Great Northern war. Ended Sweden's dominance and marked Russia's rise as a major power in Eastern Europe.
May 1722	Peter the Great established the Collegium of Little Russia to monitor the Ukrainian Cossacks ("Little Russia" or "Malorussia" is a derogatory term for Ukraine).
December 1722	Hryhorii Skovoroda was born.
February 1725	Peter The Great died.
1735-1739	Cossacks had to fight for the Russian Empire in the Russo-Turkish War.
July 1762	Catherine The Great acceded to the throne.
November 1764	By the order of Empress Catherine II, Hetmanate was abolished, and Little Russia Governorate was established.
1768	Koliyivshchina- a Cossack-peasant uprising in Right-Bank Ukraine against Polish rule, driven by social and religious oppression, and was violently suppressed.
1772	The First Partition of Poland. The Austrian Empire annexed Galicia.
September 1773- Summer of 1775	Pugachev's Rebellion.
July 1774	The Treaty of Küçük Kaynarca ended the Russo-Turkish War, giving Russia Black Sea access and weakening Ottoman power.
1775	Catherine The Great ordered the destruction of the Zaporizhzhian Sich.
4 July 1776	The United States of America declared its independence.
April 1783	The Crimean Khanate was defeated and annexed by the Russian Empire.
1789 - 1799	French Revolution. Slave rebellion in the French colony of Haiti, declared independence in 1804.

1793	The Russian Empire annexed eastern Ukraine during the Second Partition of Poland.
1794	Odessa was officially founded as a city by the Russian Empire.
9 November 1794	Hrihorii Skovoroda died.
1795	Ukraine was divided between the Russian and Austrian Empires in the Third Partition of Poland.
17 November 1796	Catherine The Great died.
1798	Ivan Kotlyarevsky publishes Eneida, the first literary work published wholly in the modern Ukrainian language.
November 1804	Kharkiv Imperial University was founded.
1812	Napoleon was defeated in his Russian campaign and withdrew from the Russian Empire.
1818	Publication of the first (modern) Ukrainian grammar *Gramatika by A. Pavlovsky (Grammar* of old Ukrainian was published by M. Smotrytsky in 1619).
27 of December 1822	Louis Pasteur was born.
1830 -1831	Polish uprising against Russian rule. Inspired national movements across Eastern Europe, including Ukraine.
15 of July 1834	Foundation of the Kyiv University.
1840	Taras Shevchenko published *Kobzar*, a collection of poems in Ukrainian.
3 (15) of May 1845	Ilya Mechnikov was born.
April 1847	Taras Shevchenko and historian Mykola Kostomarov were arrested and convicted for their participation in the Kyrylo-Mefodii Brotherhood, aimed at Ukraine's independence,
1848	The February Revolution in France inspired a revolutionary movement (Spring of the Nations) in Galicia, and a decree for the emancipation of serfs was issued in the Austrian Empire.
1848	Karl Marx and Friedrich Engels wrote *Communist Manifesto*.
1856	The Crimean War ended, and Russia lost its Black Sea Fleet.
1859	Charles Darwin wrote *The Origin of Species*.
1860	The Russian Empire established the city of Vladivostok in the Far East.
1861	Serfdom was abolished in the Russian Empire.

Historical Timeline 163

1863	The Valuev Circular (Russian Minister of the Interior) banned Ukrainian-language publications and plays.
1863-1864	The Polish uprising inspired Ukrainian national consciousness but triggered increased Russian repression in Ukrainian territories.
July 1868	Establishment of the Prosvita association in Galicia, aimed at the enlightenment of the Ukrainian people.
1868	Meiji Restoration in Japan.
1874-1875	Leo Mechnikov, the brother of Ilia Mechnikov, stayed in Japan.
May 1876	Russia issued the Ems Ukaz (Law), banning the use of Ukrainian language in prints, plays and lectures in Ukrainian, as well as import of Ukrainian language prints.
February 1877	Serhii Bortkevych/Sergei Bortkiewicz was born.
1877-1878	Russo-Turkish War.
1883	Ilia Mechnikov publishes his phagocytosis theory.
November 1885	Sarah Shtern (Sonia Delaunay) was born.
March 1886	Mykhailo Tereshchenko was born.
1886	Konishi Masutaro studied at the Kyiv Theological Seminary.
May 1889	Igor Sikorsky was born.
1890	The first modern Ukrainian political party, Ruthenian-Ukrainian Radical Party, was formed in Galicia.
1890	Senuma Kakusaburo studied at the Kyiv Theological Seminary.
1891-1904	The construction of the Siberian Railway.
1893	Pyotr (Petro) Tchaikovsky died.
February 1895	Archduke Wilhelm Franz of Austria (Vasyl Vyshyvanyi) was born.
1895	Luis Pasteur died.
April 1897	Ivan Svit was born.
1897	Stepan Levynskyi was born (exact date unknown).
1898	Kyiv Polytechnic Institute was founded.
1900	The first political party in Ukraine under the Russian Empire, the Ukrainian Revolutionary Party, was formed.
1903	The Wright Brothers made their first successful piloted flight.
1904-1905	The Russo-Japanese War.

1905	The establishment of a parliament was promulgated in Russia in response to the nationwide expansion of protests against the Czarist regime.
1905	First Revolution in the Russian Empire. The October Proclamation of Nicholas II abolished the Ems Law.
1906	Pyotr Stolypin became Prime Minister.
May 1907	Sofia (Sophie) Yablonska was born.
1908	Ilia Mechnikov was awarded the Nobel Prize in Physiology and Medicine.
1911	Pyotr Stolypin was assassinated in the Kyiv Opera theatre.
1911	Guillaume Apollinaire wrote *Le Bestiaire ou Cortège d'Orphée*.
1914	Outbreak of World War I.
July 1916	Ilia Mechnikov died.
February/March 1917	The February Revolution in Russia abolished the Czarist regime and established a provisional government. Mykhailo Tereshchenko joined the Russian provisional government.
1917	The Bolshevik Party seized power in the October Revolution and started the invasion of Ukraine.
22 of January 1918	Ukrainian Central Rada declared the independence of the Ukrainian People's Republic and signed its own peace treaties with the belligerents of World War I.
1918	The movement for Ukrainian independence grows in the Far East.
1918-1922	Foreign intervention against the Bolshevik regime in the Far East. Japan also sent troops to Siberia.
April- December 1918	Ukrainian state and Skoropadsky government in Kyiv.
November 1918	The Directorate of Ukraine was established in place of the Central Rada government.
22 January 1919	Unification of Eastern and Western Ukraine.
28 June 1919	Treaty of Versailles ended WWI.
1920	Bolsheviks took over most of the Ukrainian territories.
18 March of 1921	The Treaty of Riga / Peace of Riga. Ended the Polish-Soviet War by dividing contested lands, with Ukraine split between Poland (western part) and Soviet Russia, crushing hopes for Ukrainian independence.

Historical Timeline 165

30 December 1922	The Union of Soviet Socialist Republics (USSR) was established.
1 March 1932	The establishment of Manchukuo.
1932-1933	Holodomor in Ukraine
1933	Hitler seizes power in Germany.
1937	The Sino-Japanese War entered into full scale.
May-November 1937	The World's Fair was held in Paris, and the colossal frescoes by the Delaunay couple were exhibited.
12 March 1938	German troops invaded Vienna.
1938	Nikita Khrushchev became First Secretary of the Communist Party of Ukraine.
August-September 1939	The German-Soviet Pact was signed in August and on 1st of September 1939 German troops invaded Poland (start of World War II).
May-June 1940	German troops invaded France.
22, June 1941	German troops invaded the Soviet Union. Soviet German war
6 June 1944	D-Day — Allied troops landed in Normandy and liberated Paris from Germany.
April 1945	Soviet troops advanced on Berlin and Vienna, and Germany and Italy surrendered one after another.
2 September 1945	Japan capitulated.
1946	British Prime Minister Winston Churchill delivered his "Iron Curtain" speech.
October 1946	Stepan Levynskyi died.
1946	The Indochina Wars begins.
February 1948	Archduke Wilhelm Franz of Austria (Vasyl Vyshyvanyi) died.
October 1952	Serhii Bortkevych/Sergei Bortkiewicz died.
1953	Death of Stalin.
7 May 1954	France withdrew from Indochina.
27 July 1955	The occupation of Vienna by the Allies ended.
25 February 1956	Nikita Khrushchev delivered a secret report at XXth Congress of the Communist Party of Soviet Union criticising Stalin and his regime.
April 1956	Mykhailo Tereshchenko died.
1958-1961	Great Leap Forward policy in China and the Great Famine.
1 January 1959	Cuban Revolution.

1960	France recognised the independence of 13 African colonies (Year of Africa).
April 1961	Yurii Gagarin's space flight.
16-28 October 1962	Cuban Crisis.
October 1964	Dismissal of Khrushchev and appointment of Brezhnev as his successor.
1964	Sonia Delaunay's solo exhibition at the Museum of Louvre.
1965-1975	The Vietnam War.
20 July 1969	Apollo 11 lands on the moon.
February 1971	Sofia (Sophie) Yablonska died.
October 1972	Igor Sikorsky died.
1976-1981	Establishment of the Ukrainian Helsinki Group, a human rights organisation, operating under Soviet repression.
December 1979	Sonia Delaunay died.
March 1985	Mikhail Gorbachev becomes General Secretary of the Communist Party of the USSR.
26 April 1986	Chornobyl nuclear power plant accident.
March 1989	Ivan Svit died.
19-21 August 1991	August Coup.
24 August- 26 1991	Ukraine declared independence. Collapse of the Soviet Union.

Selected Bibliography

Introduction

Magocsi, Paul Robert. *A History of Ukraine: The Land and Its Peoples*. Toronto: University of Toronto Press, 2010.

Subtelny, Orest. *Ukraine: A History*. Toronto: University of Toronto Press, 1988.

Hryhorii Skovoroda

Fukuzawa, Yukichi. *An Encouragement of Learning*. Translated by David A. Dilworth and Umeyo Hirano. Tokyo: Keio University Press, 2008.

Fukuzawa, Yukichi. *The Autobiography of Yukichi Fukuzawa*. Translated by Eiichi Kiyooka. New York: Columbia University Press, 1966.

Fukuzawa, Yukichi. *An Outline of a Theory of Civilization*. Translated by David A. Dilworth and G. Cameron Hurst. New York: Columbia University Press, 2009.

Skovoroda, Hryhorii. *Povne zibrannia tvoriv u dvokh tomakh*. Edited by Volodymyr Ivanovych Shynkaruk, Ivan Vasyliovych Ivanenko, and others. Kyiv: Naukova Dumka, 1973.

Skovoroda, Hryhory. *The Garden of Divine Songs and Collected Poetry of Hryhory Skovoroda*. Translated by Michael M. Naydan. Introduction by Valery Shevchuk. Edited by Olha Tytarenko. London: Glagoslav Publications, 2016.

Ilya Mechnikov

Konishi, Sho. Anarchist Modernity: Cooperatism and Japanese-Russian Intellectual Relations in Modern Japan. Harvard East Asian Monographs 356. Cambridge, MA: Harvard University Press, 2013.

Metchnikoff, Élie. The Prolongation of Life: Optimistic Studies: Unlocking the Secrets of Longevity: A Scientific Journey. Edited by Peter Chalmers Mitchell. Good Press, 2019.

Metchnikoff, Élie. Chōju no Kenkyū: Rakkanronsha no Essei. Tokyo: Kōshobō, 2006.

Metchnikoff, Élie. Kindai Igaku no Kensetsusha. Translated by Sadao Miyamura. Tokyo: Iwanami Bunko, 1968.

Mogilevsky, Boris. Ilya Ilyich Mechnikov. Moscow: Molodaya Gvardiya, 1958.

Reznik, Sergei. Mechnikov. Moscow: Molodaya Gvardiya, 1973.

Solovieva, Olga, and Sho Konishi. Japan's Russia: Challenging the East-West Paradigm. Amherst, MA: Cambria Press, 2021.

Zalkind, Solomon. Ilya Mechnikov: His Life and Work. Honolulu: University Press of the Pacific, 2001.

Serhii Bortkevych / Sergei Bortkiewicz

Bortkiewicz: Piano Works. Performed by Pavel Gintov. Piano Classics (Brilliant Classics), 2017. Compact disc.

Čajkovskij, Pëtr Il'ič. Briefwechsel Peter Tschaikowsky's mit Frau Nadjeschda von Meck. Translated from Russian by Sergei Bortkiewicz. Leipzig: Koehler & Amelang, 1938.

Coombs, Stephen. "Sergei Bortkiewicz (1877–1952) on Hyperion Records." Hyperion Records, 2000. https://www.hyperion-records.co.uk/c.asp?c=C79.

Hryshchenko, Alexis. Between East and West: Memoirs, Notes, Essays. New York: The Ukrainian Academy of Arts and Sciences in the U.S., 1954.

Kalkman, Willem. "Sergei Bortkiewicz: His Life and Music." Last modified July 31, 2015. https://sergeibortkiewicz.com/.

Sonia Delaunay

Asakura, Mie. Sonia Delaunay: Fukushoku Geijutsu no Tanjō. Tokyo: Buryukke, 2010.

Delaunay, Sonia. Tapis et tissus. Paris: Éditions d'Art Charles Moreau, c. 1929.

Delaunay, Sonia. Compositions, couleurs, idées. Paris: Éditions d'Art Charles Moreau, c. 1930.

Madsen, Axel. Sonia Delaunay: Artist of the Lost Generation. New York: McGraw-Hill, 1989.

Manes, Cara. Sonia Delaunay: A Life of Color. Illustrated by Fatinha Ramos. New York: Harry N. Abrams, 2017.

Montfort, Alvaro, and Cécile Godefroy. Sonia Delaunay. London: Tate Gallery Publishing, 2014.

Takehara, Akiko. Sonia Delaunay: Pari Dezain-kai o Rīdo shita Gaka. Tokyo: Saijusha, 1995.

Mykhailo Tereshchenko

Tereshchenko, Michelle. *Pershyi oliharkh Mykhailo Ivanovych Tereshchenko 1886–1956: Nadzvychaina istoriia zhyttia moho dida, yak yii rozpovila meni moia babusia.* Translated from French by Tetiana Tsymbal. Kyiv: Nika-Tsentr, 2013.

Tereshchenko, Michelle. *V poiskakh klada semi Tereshchenko.* Translated from French by Tetiana Tsymbal. Kyiv: Nika-Tsentr, 2012.

Igor Sikorsky

Shpak, Ihor. *Igor Sikorskyi: Vid Kyieva do Konnektikuta, Vid Neba do Nebes.* Kyiv: ADEF-Ukraina, 2015.

Sikorsky, Sergei. *The Sikorsky Legacy (Images of Aviation).* Portland, OR: Book News, 2009.

Sikorsky, Igor Ivanovich, Jr. *The Lindbergh-Sikorsky Connection.* New York: Page Publishing, 2021.

Ivan Svit

Chornomaz, Vyacheslav, ed. *Ukrainci v Kytai: entsyklopedychnyi dovidnyk [Ukrainians in China: Encyclopedic Reference].* Odesa: Helvetyka, 2021.

Khomenko, Olga. *Dalekoskhidna Odisseia Ivana Svita.* Kyiv: Laurus, 2021.

Khomenko, Olga. "The Enemy of My Enemy Is My Friend: Ukrainian-Japanese Cooperation in Manchuria against the Soviet Union (1932–1945)." *Kamizono, Journal of the Meiji Jingu Intercultural Research Institute* 32 (November 2024): 199–210.

Khomenko, Olga. "Higashi Ajia no naka no Ukuraina: Iwan Svitt no ashiato o otte." *Roshia Bunka Tsūshin Gun* 54 (2019): 3. Gunzōsha.

Konishi, Sho. *Anarchist Modernity: Cooperatism and Japanese–Russian Intellectual Relations in Modern Japan.* Cambridge, MA: Harvard University Asia Centre, 2013.

Mandzurskiy Vistnyk, March 21, 1937.

Mapa Zelenoi Ukraini [Map of Green Ukraine]. Harbin, 1937.

Nakai, Kazuo. "Amerika no naka no Ukuraina, soshite Nihon." *Mado* 45 (1983): 14–19. Nauka.

Okabe, Yoshihiko. *Nihon Ukuraina Kōryū-shi 1915–1937-nen.* Kōbe: Kōbe Gakuin Daigaku Shuppankai, 2021.

Svit, Ivan. *Ukrainsko-iaponski vzaiemyny 1903–1945 (Istorychnyi ohliad ta sposterezhennia).* New York: Ukrainske Istorychne Tovarystvo, 1972.

Svit, Ivan. *Skorochena Istoriya Ukrainskogo Rukhu na Dalekomu Skhodi (Asia).* Written in 1938. First published in Olga Khomenko, *Dalekoskhidna Odisseia Ivana Svita*, 208–410. Kyiv: Laurus, 2021.

Tōa seijō [*The Political Situation in East Asia*]. Edited by Manchukuo Ministry of Foreign Affairs, 1936. "Ukuraina undō gaiken" [An Overview of the Ukrainian Movement]. *Shinto* 5: 39–72.

Furusawa, Kōkichi. *Kōkichi Furusawa Jiden "Waga-ya no Kiroku": Murakami, Akkeshi, Tokyo, Harbin* [*Autobiography of Kōkichi Furusawa: Record of My Family – Murakami, Akkeshi, Tokyo, Harbin*]. 2016.

Stepan Levynskyi

Levynskyi, Stepan. *Vid Vezuviia do piskiv Sakhary. Z yaponskoho domu. Skhid i Zakhid.* Lviv: LA Piramida, 2018.

Levynskyi, Stepan. *Paryzki nastroi.* Lviv: LA Piramida, 2020.

Interview with Mayotte Magnus-Lewinska, Alan. July 28, 2025.

Sofia Yablonska-Oudin

Yablonska, Sofia. *Char Maroka.* Kyiv: Rodovid, 2018.

Yablonska, Sofia. *Z krainy ryzhu ta opiiu.* Kyiv: Rodovid, 2018.

Yablonska, Sofia. *Knyha pro batka. Z moho dytynstva.* Kyiv: Bohuslavknyha, 2015.

Yablonska, Sofia. *Lysty z Paryzha. Lysty z Kytaiu. Podorozhni narysy, novely, esei, intervju.* Edited and annotated by Volodymyr Gabor. Lviv: LA Piramida, 2018.

Zabuzhko, Oksana. "Kilka urokiv vid Sofii Yablonskoi." In *Planeta Polyn: Vybrani Esei*, 73–90. Kyiv: Komora, 2020.

Zabuzhko, Oksana. *Teura. Sofiia Yablonska.* Kyiv: Rodovid, 2018.

Vasyl Vyshyvanyi

Andriushchenko, Eduard. "Herzog and Spy in a Kyiv Prison: The Case of Vasyl Vyshyvanyi." *Istorychna Pravda*, May 20, 2020.

Snyder, Timothy. *The Red Prince: The Secret Lives of a Habsburg Archduke.* New York: Basic Books, 2010.

Tsalyk, Stanislav. "Vasyl Vyshyvanyi: The Austrian Archduke Who Could Have Become Hetman of Ukraine." *BBC Ukrainian*, August 18, 2017.

Epilogue

Bhabha, Homi K. *The Location of Culture*. London: Routledge, 1994.

Hall, Stuart. "Cultural Identity and Diaspora." In *Identity: Community, Culture, Difference*, edited by Jonathan Rutherford. London: Lawrence & Wishart, 1990.

Lyotard, Jean-François. *The Postmodern Condition: A Report on Knowledge*. 1979; English translation, 1984.

Pratt, Mary Louise. "Arts of the Contact Zone." *Profession* (1991): 33–40.

Pratt, Mary Louise. *Imperial Eyes: Travel Writing and Transculturation*. 2nd ed. London: Routledge, 2008.

UKRAINIAN VOICES

Collected by Andreas Umland

1. *Mychailo Wynnyckyj*
   Ukraine's Maidan, Russia's War
   A Chronicle and Analysis of the Revolution of Dignity
   With a foreword by Serhii Plokhy
   ISBN 978-3-8382-1327-9

2. *Olexander Hryb*
   Understanding Contemporary Ukrainian and Russian Nationalism
   The Post-Soviet Cossack Revival and Ukraine's National Security
   With a foreword by Vitali Vitaliev
   ISBN 978-3-8382-1377-4

3. *Marko Bojcun*
   Towards a Political Economy of Ukraine
   Selected Essays 1990–2015
   With a foreword by John-Paul Himka
   ISBN 978-3-8382-1368-2

4. *Volodymyr Yermolenko (ed.)*
   Ukraine in Histories and Stories
   Essays by Ukrainian Intellectuals
   With a preface by Peter Pomerantsev
   ISBN 978-3-8382-1456-6

5. *Mykola Riabchuk*
   At the Fence of Metternich's Garden
   Essays on Europe, Ukraine, and Europeanization
   ISBN 978-3-8382-1484-9

6. *Marta Dyczok*
   Ukraine Calling
   A Kaleidoscope from Hromadske Radio 2016–2019
   With a foreword by Andriy Kulykov
   ISBN 978-3-8382-1472-6

7. *Olexander Scherba*
   Ukraine vs. Darkness
   Undiplomatic Thoughts
   With a foreword by Adrian Karatnycky
   ISBN 978-3-8382-1501-3

8. *Olesya Yaremchuk*
   Our Others
   Stories of Ukrainian Diversity
   With a foreword by Ostap Slyvynsky
   Translated from the Ukrainian by Zenia Tompkins and Hanna Leliv
   ISBN 978-3-8382-1475-7

9. *Nataliya Gumenyuk*
   Die verlorene Insel
   Geschichten von der besetzten Krim
   Mit einem Vorwort von Alice Bota
   Aus dem Ukrainischen übersetzt von Johann Zajaczkowski
   ISBN 978-3-8382-1499-3

10. *Olena Stiazhkina*
    Zero Point Ukraine
    Four Essays on World War II
    Translated from the Ukrainian by Svitlana Kulinska
    ISBN 978-3-8382-1550-1

11 *Oleksii Sinchenko, Dmytro Stus, Leonid Finberg (compilers)*
 Ukrainian Dissidents
 An Anthology of Texts
 ISBN 978-3-8382-1551-8

12 *John-Paul Himka*
 Ukrainian Nationalists and the Holocaust
 OUN and UPA's Participation in the Destruction of Ukrainian Jewry, 1941–1944
 ISBN 978-3-8382-1548-8

13 *Andrey Demartino*
 False Mirrors
 The Weaponization of Social Media in Russia's Operation to Annex Crimea
 With a foreword by Oleksiy Danilov
 ISBN 978-3-8382-1533-4

14 *Svitlana Biedarieva (ed.)*
 Contemporary Ukrainian and Baltic Art
 Political and Social Perspectives, 1991–2021
 ISBN 978-3-8382-1526-6

15 *Olesya Khromeychuk*
 A Loss
 The Story of a Dead Soldier Told by His Sister
 With a foreword by Andrey Kurkov
 ISBN 978-3-8382-1570-9

16 *Marieluise Beck (Hg.)*
 Ukraine verstehen
 Auf den Spuren von Terror und Gewalt
 Mit einem Vorwort von Dmytro Kuleba
 ISBN 978-3-8382-1653-9

17 *Stanislav Aseyev*
 Heller Weg
 Geschichte eines Konzentrationslagers im Donbass 2017–2019
 Aus dem Russischen übersetzt von Martina Steis und Charis Haska
 ISBN 978-3-8382-1620-1

18 *Mykola Davydiuk*
 Wie funktioniert Putins Propaganda?
 Anmerkungen zum Informationskrieg des Kremls
 Aus dem Ukrainischen übersetzt von Christian Weise
 ISBN 978-3-8382-1628-7

19 *Olesya Yaremchuk*
 Unsere Anderen
 Geschichten ukrainischer Vielfalt
 Aus dem Ukrainischen übersetzt von Christian Weise
 ISBN 978-3-8382-1635-5

20 *Oleksandr Mykhed*
 „Dein Blut wird die Kohle tränken"
 Über die Ostukraine
 Aus dem Ukrainischen übersetzt von Simon Muschick und Dario Planert
 ISBN 978-3-8382-1648-5

21 *Vakhtang Kipiani (Hg.)*
 Der Zweite Weltkrieg in der Ukraine
 Geschichte und Lebensgeschichten
 Aus dem Ukrainischen übersetzt von Margarita Grinko
 ISBN 978-3-8382-1622-5

22 *Vakhtang Kipiani (ed.)*
 World War II, Uncontrived and Unredacted
 Testimonies from Ukraine
 Translated from the Ukrainian by Zenia Tompkins and Daisy Gibbons
 ISBN 978-3-8382-1621-8

23 **Dmytro Stus**
Vasyl Stus
Life in Creativity
Translated from the Ukrainian by
Ludmila Bachurina
ISBN 978-3-8382-1631-7

24 **Vitalii Ogiienko (ed.)**
The Holodomor and the
Origins of the Soviet Man
Reading the Testimony of
Anastasia Lysyvets
With forewords by Natalka
Bilotserkivets and Serhy
Yekelchyk
Translated from the Ukrainian by
Alla Parkhomenko and
Alexander J. Motyl
ISBN 978-3-8382-1616-4

25 **Vladislav Davidzon**
Jewish-Ukrainian Relations
and the Birth of a Political
Nation
Selected Writings 2013-2021
With a foreword by Bernard-
Henri Lévy
ISBN 978-3-8382-1509-9

26 **Serhy Yekelchyk**
Writing the Nation
The Ukrainian Historical
Profession in Independent
Ukraine and the Diaspora
ISBN 978-3-8382-1695-9

27 **Ildi Eperjesi, Oleksandr Kachura**
Shreds of War
Fates from the Donbas Frontline
2014-2019
With a foreword by Olexiy
Haran
ISBN 978-3-8382-1680-5

28 **Oleksandr Melnyk**
World War II as an Identity
Project
Historicism, Legitimacy
Contests, and the (Re-)Construction of Political Communities in Ukraine, 1939–1946
With a foreword by David R.
Marples
ISBN 978-3-8382-1704-8

29 **Olesya Khromeychuk**
Ein Verlust
Die Geschichte eines gefallenen
ukrainischen Soldaten, erzählt
von seiner Schwester
Mit einem Vorwort von Andrej
Kurkow
Aus dem Englischen übersetzt
von Lily Sophie
ISBN 978-3-8382-1770-3

30 **Tamara Martsenyuk, Tetiana Kostiuchenko (eds.)**
Russia's War in Ukraine
During 2022
Personal Experiences of
Ukrainian Scholars
ISBN 978-3-8382-1757-4

31 **Ildikó Eperjesi, Oleksandr Kachura**
Shreds of War. Vol. 2
Fates from Crimea 2015–2022
With an interview of Oleh
Sentsov
ISBN 978-3-8382-1780-2

32 **Yuriy Lukanov**
The Press
How Russia Destroyed Media
Freedom in Crimea
With a foreword by Taras Kuzio
ISBN 978-3-8382-1784-0

33 **Megan Buskey**
Ukraine Is Not Dead Yet
A Family Story of Exile and
Return
ISBN 978-3-8382-1691-1

34 *Vira Ageyeva*
Behind the Scenes of the Empire
Essays on Cultural Relationships between Ukraine and Russia
With a foreword by Oksana Zabuzhko
ISBN 978-3-8382-1748-2

35 *Marieluise Beck (ed.)*
Understanding Ukraine
Tracing the Roots of Terror and Violence
With a foreword by Dmytro Kuleba
ISBN 978-3-8382-1773-4

36 *Olesya Khromeychuk*
A Loss
The Story of a Dead Soldier Told by His Sister, 2nd edn.
With a foreword by Philippe Sands
With a preface by Andrii Kurkov
ISBN 978-3-8382-1870-0

37 *Taras Kuzio, Stefan Jajecznyk-Kelman*
Fascism and Genocide
Russia's War Against Ukrainians
ISBN 978-3-8382-1791-8

38 *Alina Nychyk*
Ukraine Vis-à-Vis Russia and the EU
Misperceptions of Foreign Challenges in Times of War, 2014–2015
With a foreword by Paul D'Anieri
ISBN 978-3-8382-1767-3

39 *Sasha Dovzhyk (ed.)*
Ukraine Lab
Global Security, Environment, and Disinformation Through the Prism of Ukraine
With a foreword by Rory Finnin
ISBN 978-3-8382-1805-2

40 *Serhiy Kvit*
Media, History, and Education
Three Ways to Ukrainian Independence
With a preface by Diane Francis
ISBN 978-3-8382-1807-6

41 *Anna Romandash*
Women of Ukraine
Reportages from the War and Beyond
ISBN 978-3-8382-1819-9

42 *Dominika Rank*
Matzewe in meinem Garten
Abenteuer eines jüdischen Heritage-Touristen in der Ukraine
ISBN 978-3-8382-1810-6

43 *Myroslaw Marynowytsch*
Das Universum hinter dem Stacheldraht
Memoiren eines sowjet-ukrainischen Dissidenten
Mit einem Vorwort von Timothy Snyder und einem Nachwort von Max Hartmann
ISBN 978-3-8382-1806-9

44 *Konstantin Sigow*
Für Deine und meine Freiheit
Europäische Revolutions- und Kriegserfahrungen im heutigen Kyjiw
Mit einem Vorwort von Karl Schlögel
Herausgegeben von Regula M. Zwahlen
ISBN 978-3-8382-1755-0

45 *Kateryna Pylypchuk*
The War that Changed Us
Ukrainian Novellas, Poems, and Essays from 2022
With a foreword by Victor Yushchenko
Paperback
ISBN 978-3-8382-1859-5
Hardcover
ISBN 978-3-8382-1860-1

46 *Kyrylo Tkachenko*
Rechte Tür Links
Radikale Linke in Deutschland, die Revolution und der Krieg in der Ukraine, 2013-2018
ISBN 978-3-8382-1711-6

47 *Alexander Strashny*
The Ukrainian Mentality
An Ethno-Psychological, Historical and Comparative Exploration
With a foreword by Antonina Lovochkina
Translated from the Ukrainian by Michael M. Naydan and Olha Tytarenko
ISBN 978-3-8382-1886-1

48 *Alona Shestopalova*
From Screens to Battlefields
Tracing the Construction of Enemies on Russian Television
With a foreword by Nina Jankowicz
ISBN 978-3-8382-1884-7

49 *Iaroslav Petik*
Politics and Society in the Ukrainian People's Republic (1917–1921) and Contemporary Ukraine (2013–2022)
A Comparative Analysis
With a foreword by Mykola Doroshko
ISBN 978-3-8382-1817-5

50 *Serhii Plokhy*
Der Mann mit der Giftpistole
Eine Spionagegeschichte aus dem Kalten Krieg
ISBN 978-3-8382-1789-5

51 *Vakhtang Kipiani*
Ukrainische Dissidenten unter der Sowjetmacht
Im Kampf um Wahrheit und Freiheit
Aus dem Ukrainischen übersetzt von Christian Weise
ISBN 978-3-8382-1890-8

52 *Dmytro Shestakov*
When Businesses Test Hypotheses
A Four-Step Approach to Risk Management for Innovative Startups
With a foreword by Anthony J. Tether
ISBN 978-3-8382-1883-0

53 *Larissa Babij*
A Kind of Refugee
The Story of an American Who Refused to Leave Ukraine
With a foreword by Vladislav Davidzon
ISBN 978-3-8382-1898-4

54 *Julia Davis*
In Their Own Words
How Russian Propagandists Reveal Putin's Intentions
With a foreword by Timothy Snyder
ISBN 978-3-8382-1909-7

55 *Sonya Atlantova, Oleksandr Klymenko*
Icons on Ammo Boxes
Painting Life on the Remnants of Russia's War in Donbas, 2014-21
Translated from the Ukrainian by Anastasya Knyazhytska
ISBN 978-3-8382-1892-2

56 *Leonid Ushkalov*
Catching an Elusive Bird
The Life of Hryhorii Skovoroda
Translated from the Ukrainian by Natalia Komarova
ISBN 978-3-8382-1894-6

57 *Vakhtang Kipiani*
Ein Land weiblichen Geschlechts
Ukrainische Frauenschicksale im 20. und 21. Jahrhundert
Aus dem Ukrainischen übersetzt von Christian Weise
ISBN 978-3-8382-1891-5

58 Petro Rychlo
„Zerrissne Saiten einer
überlauten Harfe ..."
Deutschjüdische Dichter der
Bukowina
ISBN 978-3-8382-1893-9

59 Volodymyr Paniotto
Sociology in Jokes
An Entertaining Introduction
ISBN 978-3-8382-1857-1

60 Josef Wallmannsberger
(ed.)
Executing Renaissances
The Poetological Nation of
Ukraine
ISBN 978-3-8382-1741-3

61 Pavlo Kazarin
The Wild West of Eastern
Europe
A Ukrainian Guide on Breaking
Free from Empire
Translated from the Ukrainian
by Dominique Hoffman
ISBN 978-3-8382-1842-7

62 Ernest Gyidel
Ukrainian Public
Nationalism in the General
Government
The Case of *Krakivski Visti*,
1940–1944
With a foreword by David R.
Marples
ISBN 978-3-8382-1865-6

63 Olexander Hryb
Understanding
Contemporary Russian
Militarism
From Revolutionary to New
Generation Warfare
With a foreword by Mark Laity
ISBN 978-3-8382-1927-1

64 Orysia Hrudka, Bohdan Ben
Dark Days, Determined
People
Stories from Ukraine under Siege
With a foreword by Myroslav
Marynovych
ISBN 978-3-8382-1958-5

65 Oleksandr Pankieiev (ed.)
Narratives of the Russo-
Ukrainian War
A Look Within and Without
With a foreword by Natalia
Khanenko-Friesen
ISBN 978-3-8382-1964-6

66 Roman Sohn, Ariana Gic
(eds.)
Unrecognized War
The Fight for Truth about
Russia's War on Ukraine
With a foreword by Viktor
Yushchenko
ISBN 978-3-8382-1947-9

67 Paul Robert Magocsi
Ukraina Redux
Schon wieder die Ukraine ...
ISBN 978-3-8382-1942-4

68 Paul Robert Magocsi
L'Ucraina Ritrovata
Sullo Stato e l'Identità Nazionale
ISBN 978-3-8382-1982-0

69 Max Hartmann
Ein Schrei der Verzweiflung
Aquarelle von Danylo Movchan
zu Russlands Krieg in der
Ukraine
Mit einem Vorwort von Mateusz
Sora
Paperback
ISBN 978-3-8382-2011-6
Hardcover
ISBN 978-3-8382-2012-3

70 Vakhtang Kebuladze (Hg.)
Die Zukunft, die wir uns
wünschen
Essays aus der Ukraine
ISBN 978-3-8382-1531-0

71 *Marieluise Beck, Jan Claas Behrends, Gelinada Grinchenko und Oksana Mikheieva (Hgg.)*
Deutsch-ukrainische Geschichten
Bruchstücke aus einer gemeinsamen Vergangenheit
ISBN 978-3-8382-2053-6

72 *Pavlo Kazarin*
Der Wilde Westen Ost-Europas
Der ukrainische Weg aus dem Imperium
Aus dem Ukrainischen übersetzt von Christian Weise
ISBN 978-3-8382-1843-4

73 *Radomyr Mokryk*
Die ukrainischen »Sechziger«
Chronologie einer Revolte
ISBN 978-3-8382-1873-1

74 *Leonid Finberg*
My Ukraine
Rethinking the Past, Building the Present
ISBN 978-3-8382-1974-5

75 *Joseph Zissels*
Consider My Inmost Thoughts
Essays, Lectures, and Interviews on Ukrainian Matters at the Turn of the Century
ISBN 978-3-8382-1975-2

76 *Margarita Yehorchenko, Iryna Berlyand, Ihor Vinokurov (eds.)*
Jewish Addresses in Ukraine
A Guide-Book
With a foreword by Leonid Finberg
ISB 978-3-8382-1976-9

77 *Viktoriia Grivina*
Kharkiv—A War City
A Collection of Essays from 2022–23
ISBN 978-3-8382-1988-2

78 *Hjørdis Clemmensen, Viktoriia Grivina, Vasylysa Shchogoleva*
Kharkiv Is a Dream
Public Art and Activism 2013–2023
With a foreword by Bohdan Volynskyi
ISBN 978-3-8382-2005-5

79 *Olga Khomenko*
The Faraway Sky of Kyiv
Ukrainians in the War
With a foreword by Hiroaki Kuromiya
ISBN 978-3-8382-2006-2

80 *Daria Mattingly, Jonathon Vsetecka (eds.)*
The Holodomor in Global Perspective
How the Famine in Ukraine Shaped the World
With a foreword by Anne Applebaum
ISBN 978-3-8382-1953-0

81 *Olga Khomenko*
Ukrainians beyond Borders
Nine Life Journeys Through the History of Eastern Europe
With a foreword by Zbigniew Wojnowski
ISBN 978-3-8382-2007-9

82 *Mykhailo Minakov*
From Servant to Leader
Chronicles of Ukraine under the Zelensky Presidency, 2019–2024
With a foreword by John Lloyd
ISBN 978-3-8382-2002-4

83 *Volodymyr Hromov (ed.)*
A Ruined Home
Sketches of War, 2022–2023
ISBN 978-3-8382-2008-6

84 Olha Tatokhina (ed.)
Why Do They Kill Our People?
Russia's War Against Ukraine as
Told by Ukrainians
With a foreword by Volodymyr
Yermolenko
ISBN 978-3-8382-2056-7

85 Mieste Hotopp-Riecke,
Sarah Reinke (Hgg.)
Die Krimtataren
Geschichte – Kultur – Politik
Mit einem Vorwort von
Nariman Dschelal
ISBN 978-3-8382-1986-8

86 Max Hartmann (ed.)
A Cry of Despair
Danylo Movchan's Watercolors
on the War in Ukraine
With a foreword by John A.
Kohan and Matheusz Sora
ISBN 978-3-8382-2051-2

87 Olha Marmilova, Yuliia
Soroka (eds.)
The Russian War Against
Ukraine
Investigations of Its Social and
Historical Context, 2014–2024
With a foreword by Ulrich
Schmid
ISBN 978-3-8382-2035-2

88 Mykola Davidyuk
How Putin's Propaganda
Works
Ukraine's Experience in Its War
Against Russia since 2014
With a foreword by Roman
Kostenko
ISBN 978-3-8382-1627-0

89 Mikhail Minakov
Der postsowjetische Mensch
Philosophische Betrachtungen
zur Gesellschaftsgeschichte nach
Ende der UdSSR
Mit einem Vorwort von Timm
Beichelt
Aus dem Englischen übersetzt
von Hermann Haushahn
ISBN 978-3-8382-2043-7

90 Serhiy Kazimir, Vahur
Laiapea
This Is How It Was
A Ukrainian Officer's 691 Days
In Russian Prisons
Translation by Tiiu Palumäe and
Ott Palumäe
ISBN 978-3-8382-2077-2

91 Anastasiia Simferovska
(ed.)
Confronting Catastrophes
The Art of Yohanan Petrovsky-
Shtern
With an introduction by Andrew
Horodysky
ISBN 978-3-8382-2163-2

92 Сергій Казимир, Вагур
Лайапеа
Так Було
691 день українського офіцера
в російських тюрмах
Переклад з російської на
українську Тетяна Лач
ISBN 978-3-8382-2177-9

93 Ilko-Sascha Kowalczuk
Freedom Shock
A Different History of East
Germany from 1989 to Today
ISBN 978-3-8382-2069-7

94 Stephen Velychenko
A Village in Revolutionary
Ukraine
How Bolshevik Rule Changed a
People: The Eyewitness Account
of a Common Man, 1918–28
With a foreword by Yaroslav
Hrytsak
ISBN 978-3-8382-2065-9

95 *Katerina Sergatskova*
Occupation and Migration in Eastern Europe
How Citizens Are Forced into Exile and Shaped by New Realities—Reports, Essays, Articles, 2014–25
With a foreword by Christopher Miller
ISBN 978-3-8382-2060-4

96 *Olena Bogatyrenko (Ed.)*
What Did Russia's Occupation of Crimea Mean?
Twelve Women Report How They Experienced the Start of the Russo-Ukrainian War in 2014
With a foreword by Olena Bogatyrenko
ISBN 978-3-8382-2092-5

97 *Larisa Kalik*
Dress Rehearsal
How Transnistria Became Russia's Roadmap for Hybrid Wars in Ukraine and Beyond
With a foreword by Francis Farrell
Translated from the Ukrainian by Kate Tsurkan
ISBN 978-3-8382-2074-1

98 *Petro Rychlo*
Regenbogen über der Donau
Studien zu ukrainisch-deutschen Literaturbeziehungen
ISBN 978-3-8382-2093-2

Book series "Ukrainian Voices"

Coordinator
Andreas Umland, National University of Kyiv-Mohyla Academy

Editorial Board
Lesia Bidochko, National University of Kyiv-Mohyla Academy
Svitlana Biedarieva, George Washington University, DC, USA
Ivan Gomza, Kyiv School of Economics, Ukraine
Natalie Jaresko, Aspen Institute, Kyiv/Washington
Olena Lennon, University of New Haven, West Haven, USA
Kateryna Yushchenko, First Lady of Ukraine 2005-2010, Kyiv
Oleksandr Zabirko, University of Regensburg, Germany

Advisory Board
Iuliia Bentia, National Academy of Arts of Ukraine, Kyiv
Natalya Belitser, Pylyp Orlyk Institute for Democracy, Kyiv
Oleksandra Bienert, Humboldt University of Berlin, Germany
Sergiy Bilenky, Canadian Institute of Ukrainian Studies, Toronto
Tymofii Brik, Kyiv School of Economics, Ukraine
Olga Brusylovska, Mechnikov National University, Odesa
Mariana Budjeryn, Harvard University, Cambridge, USA
Volodymyr Bugrov, Shevchenko National University, Kyiv
Olga Burlyuk, University of Amsterdam, The Netherlands
Yevhen Bystrytsky, NAS Institute of Philosophy, Kyiv
Andrii Danylenko, Pace University, New York, USA
Vladislav Davidzon, Atlantic Council, Washington/Paris
Mykola Davydiuk, Think Tank "Polityka," Kyiv
Andrii Demartino, National Security and Defense Council, Kyiv
Vadym Denisenko, Ukrainian Institute for the Future, Kyiv
Oleksandr Donii, Center for Political Values Studies, Kyiv
Volodymyr Dubovyk, Mechnikov National University, Odesa
Volodymyr Dubrovskiy, CASE Ukraine, Kyiv
Diana Dutsyk, National University of Kyiv-Mohyla Academy
Marta Dyczok, Western University, Ontario, Canada
Yevhen Fedchenko, National University of Kyiv-Mohyla Academy
Sofiya Filonenko, State Pedagogical University of Berdyansk
Oleksandr Fisun, Karazin National University, Kharkiv
Oksana Forostyna, Webjournal "Ukraina Moderna," Kyiv
Roman Goncharenko, Broadcaster "Deutsche Welle," Bonn
George Grabowicz, Harvard University, Cambridge, USA
Gelinada Grinchenko, Karazin National University, Kharkiv
Kateryna Härtel, Federal Union of European Nationalities, Brussels
Nataliia Hendel, University of Geneva, Switzerland
Anton Herashchenko, Kyiv School of Public Administration
John-Paul Himka, University of Alberta, Edmonton
Ola Hnatiuk, National University of Kyiv-Mohyla Academy
Oleksandr Holubov, Broadcaster "Deutsche Welle," Bonn
Yaroslav Hrytsak, Ukrainian Catholic University, Lviv
Oleksandra Humenna, National University of Kyiv-Mohyla Academy
Tamara Hundorova, NAS Institute of Literature, Kyiv
Oksana Huss, University of Bologna, Italy
Oleksandra Iwaniuk, University of Warsaw, Poland
Mykola Kapitonenko, Shevchenko National University, Kyiv
Georgiy Kasianov, Marie Curie-Skłodowska University, Lublin
Vakhtang Kebuladze, Shevchenko National University, Kyiv
Natalia Khanenko-Friesen, University of Alberta, Edmonton
Victoria Khiterer, Millersville University of Pennsylvania, USA
Oksana Kis, NAS Institute of Ethnology, Lviv
Pavlo Klimkin, Center for National Resilience and Development, Kyiv
Oleksandra Kolomiiets, Center for Economic Strategy, Kyiv

Sergiy Korsunsky, Kobe Gakuin University, Japan
Nadiia Koval, Kyiv School of Economics, Ukraine
Volodymyr Kravchenko, University of Alberta, Edmonton
Oleksiy Kresin, NAS Koretskiy Institute of State and Law, Kyiv
Anatoliy Kruglashov, Fedkovych National University, Chernivtsi
Andrey Kurkov, PEN Ukraine, Kyiv
Ostap Kushnir, Lazarski University, Warsaw
Taras Kuzio, National University of Kyiv-Mohyla Academy
Serhii Kvit, National University of Kyiv-Mohyla Academy
Yuliya Ladygina, The Pennsylvania State University, USA
Yevhen Mahda, Institute of World Policy, Kyiv
Victoria Malko, California State University, Fresno, USA
Yulia Marushevska, Security and Defense Center (SAND), Kyiv
Myroslav Marynovych, Ukrainian Catholic University, Lviv
Oleksandra Matviichuk, Center for Civil Liberties, Kyiv
Mykhailo Minakov, Kennan Institute, Washington, USA
Anton Moiseienko, The Australian National University, Canberra
Alexander Motyl, Rutgers University-Newark, USA
Vlad Mykhnenko, University of Oxford, United Kingdom
Vitalii Ogiienko, Ukrainian Institute of National Remembrance, Kyiv
Olga Onuch, University of Manchester, United Kingdom
Olesya Ostrovska, Museum "Mystetskyi Arsenal," Kyiv
Anna Osypchuk, National University of Kyiv-Mohyla Academy
Oleksandr Pankieiev, University of Alberta, Edmonton
Oleksiy Panych, Publishing House "Dukh i Litera," Kyiv
Valerii Pekar, Kyiv-Mohyla Business School, Ukraine
Yohanan Petrovsky-Shtern, Northwestern University, Chicago
Serhii Plokhy, Harvard University, Cambridge, USA
Andrii Portnov, Viadrina University, Frankfurt-Oder, Germany
Maryna Rabinovych, Kyiv School of Economics, Ukraine
Valentyna Romanova, Institute of Developing Economies, Tokyo
Natalya Ryabinska, Collegium Civitas, Warsaw, Poland

Darya Tsymbalyk, University of Oxford, United Kingdom
Vsevolod Samokhvalov, University of Liege, Belgium
Orest Semotiuk, Franko National University, Lviv
Viktoriya Sereda, NAS Institute of Ethnology, Lviv
Anton Shekhovtsov, University of Vienna, Austria
Andriy Shevchenko, Media Center Ukraine, Kyiv
Oxana Shevel, Tufts University, Medford, USA
Pavlo Shopin, National Pedagogical Dragomanov University, Kyiv
Karina Shyrokykh, Stockholm University, Sweden
Nadja Simon, freelance interpreter, Cologne, Germany
Olena Snigova, NAS Institute for Economics and Forecasting, Kyiv
Ilona Solohub, Analytical Platform "VoxUkraine," Kyiv
Iryna Solonenko, LibMod - Center for Liberal Modernity, Berlin
Galyna Solovei, National University of Kyiv-Mohyla Academy
Sergiy Stelmakh, NAS Institute of World History, Kyiv
Olena Stiazhkina, NAS Institute of the History of Ukraine, Kyiv
Dmitri Stratievski, Osteuropa Zentrum (OEZB), Berlin
Dmytro Stus, National Taras Shevchenko Museum, Kyiv
Frank Sysyn, University of Toronto, Canada
Olha Tokariuk, Center for European Policy Analysis, Washington
Olena Tregub, Independent Anti-Corruption Commission, Kyiv
Hlib Vyshlinsky, Centre for Economic Strategy, Kyiv
Mychailo Wynnyckyj, National University of Kyiv-Mohyla Academy
Yelyzaveta Yasko, NGO "Yellow Blue Strategy," Kyiv
Serhy Yekelchyk, University of Victoria, Canada
Victor Yushchenko, President of Ukraine 2005-2010, Kyiv
Oleksandr Zaitsev, Ukrainian Catholic University, Lviv
Kateryna Zarembo, National University of Kyiv-Mohyla Academy
Yaroslav Zhalilo, National Institute for Strategic Studies, Kyiv
Sergei Zhuk, Ball State University at Muncie, USA
Alina Zubkovych, Nordic Ukraine Forum, Stockholm
Liudmyla Zubrytska, National University of Kyiv-Mohyla Academy

Friends of the Series

Ana Maria Abulescu, University of Bucharest, Romania
Łukasz Adamski, Centrum Mieroszewskiego, Warsaw
Marieluise Beck, LibMod—Center for Liberal Modernity, Berlin
Marc Berensen, King's College London, United Kingdom
Johannes Bohnen, BOHNEN Public Affairs, Berlin
Karsten Brüggemann, University of Tallinn, Estonia
Ulf Brunnbauer, Leibniz Institute (IOS), Regensburg
Martin Dietze, German-Ukrainian Culture Society, Hamburg
Gergana Dimova, Florida State University, Tallahassee/London
Caroline von Gall, Goethe University, Frankfurt-Main
Zaur Gasimov, Rhenish Friedrich Wilhelm University, Bonn
Armand Gosu, University of Bucharest, Romania
Thomas Grant, University of Cambridge, United Kingdom
Gustav Gressel, European Council on Foreign Relations, Berlin
Rebecca Harms, European Centre for Press & Media Freedom, Leipzig
André Härtel, Stiftung Wissenschaft und Politik, Berlin/Brussels
Marcel Van Herpen, The Cicero Foundation, Maastricht
Richard Herzinger, freelance analyst, Berlin
Mieste Hotopp-Riecke, ICATAT, Magdeburg
Nico Lange, Munich Security Conference, Berlin
Martin Malek, freelance analyst, Vienna
Ingo Mannteufel, Broadcaster "Deutsche Welle," Bonn
Carlo Masala, Bundeswehr University, Munich
Wolfgang Mueller, University of Vienna, Austria
Dietmar Neutatz, Albert Ludwigs University, Freiburg
Torsten Oppelland, Friedrich Schiller University, Jena
Niccolò Pianciola, University of Padua, Italy
Gerald Praschl, German-Ukrainian Forum (DUF), Berlin
Felix Riefer, Think Tank Ideenagentur-Ost, Düsseldorf
Stefan Rohdewald, University of Leipzig, Germany
Sebastian Schäffer, Institute for the Danube Region (IDM), Vienna
Felix Schimansky-Geier, Friedrich Schiller University, Jena
Ulrich Schneckener, University of Osnabrück, Germany
Winfried Schneider-Deters, freelance analyst, Heidelberg/Kyiv
Gerhard Simon, University of Cologne, Germany
Kai Struve, Martin Luther University, Halle/Wittenberg
David Stulik, European Values Center for Security Policy, Prague
Andrzej Szeptycki, University of Warsaw, Poland
Philipp Ther, University of Vienna, Austria
Stefan Troebst, University of Leipzig, Germany

[Please send requests for changes in, corrections of, and additions to, this list to andreas.umland@stanforalumni.org.]

ibidem.eu